Emil Schulthess   Africa

Emil Schulthess

A

Introduction   Emil Egli
Captions   Emil Birrer
Notes   Emil Schulthess

FRICA

Collins   St. James's Place   London

By the same author: "China", "The Amazon", "Antarctica"

First British edition 1959
Second revised British edition 1969
British edition reprinted 1973
Original edition: Manesse Verlag, Zurich
Second revised edition: Artemis Verlags-AG, Zurich and Stuttgart

© 1969 Artemis Verlags-AG, Zurich and Stuttgart
© 1969 English translation: Artemis Verlags-AG, Zurich and Stuttgart
© 1969 Illustrations: Emil Schulthess
ISBN 0 00 211035 0

English Translation by Brian Battershaw and T. and K. Schelbert
Design: Emil Schulthess
Illustrations printed by gravure: Imago, Zurich
Text printed by letterpress: Regina-Druck, Zurich
Paper by Papierfabrik Biberist
Binding by Buchbinderei Burkhardt, Zurich
Printed in Switzerland

for Bruna

Publisher's Preface

When Emil Schulthess received the coveted US Camera Achievement Award in 1967, two of his books were cited as the grounds for this distinction: *Africa* and *China*. Ten years lie between the two publications, and although *Africa* has long been unobtainable, connoisseurs continue to hold it in an esteem which is in marked contrast to the ephemeral photographic reputations of our time. This is only one of the reasons why the book is now being published again in an enlarged and redesigned format.

In recent years the African continent has been in a state of social, economic and political upheaval which makes it almost impossible to offer any comment that is not instantly out of date. Nevertheless in *Africa* Emil Schulthess has managed to say something, in his own distinctive way, which is lasting.

One of the most distinguished authorities to review the original edition of the book wrote: "I cannot believe that any truer pictures of Africa have ever been taken or are likely to be taken for many a year. To open the book anywhere is to recognise the Africa one knows—even when, in fact, it may be the very remote Africa of French or Belgian Congo. This must be because the photographer has achieved that most difficult capture, the exact truth of the moment; the complete atmosphere of the place; the perfect expression whether animal or human which the picture demands.

"But, apart from the unquestionable brilliance of the photographs themselves, there are other, massive reasons why this book is worth every penny it costs. In the first place it brings home most astonishingly that truth which all of us who are striving to express the meaning of African events today *feel*, but cannot easily convey: the truth of the unity of the African continent. The great landmass from the Mediterranean to the southernmost crag of the Cape of Good Hope is one continent not merely by virtue of its formation but by virtue of its power to take hold of and influence and shape its peoples.

"Secondly, this book brings home the vastness of Africa and the way in which this vastness makes her, so to say, contemptuous of much that passes for civilisation in the West. So that, although it would have been interesting to see more photographs of urban life than here appear, it might well have been a mistake to attempt this. To those who will buy this book it is more important to show the grandeur of Africa and her peoples than it is to show at any great length the achievements of Western culture."

Today, particularly in a world which continuously disseminates falsified information in words and pictures, a statement of enduring reality is the fundamental justification for the republication of a photographic book like *Africa*. That this reality is presented in a form so beautiful further belies the so-called realism which prefers the absurd and grotesque, the shrill and sensational. For Emil Schulthess, the aesthetic approach is the only possible one, and this explains his particular attention to the colour plates. For in these, far more than in the black and white prints, his vision of reality and his concept of the universe find their truest expression.

The inimitable and lasting effect created by his pictures is attained neither by mannerism nor simply by technical expertise, but through the intensity of the relationship between the photographer and his subject. His photography represents a connection between the outer and the inner worlds, and thus produces something permanent in a pictorial form. Emil Schulthess's achievement cannot be assigned to any category, group or class—even the term photography fails to express its nature adequately. His work stands on its own, and in the hands of the reader is able to communicate its quality far better than any words.

The Continent of Africa

Only eight and a half miles of water separate the Rock of Gibraltar from the Riff Mountains. The dark continent, Africa, lies, a close neighbour, right before the southern gateway of Europe. The ancient Greeks were already feeling for its secrets. Herodotus described its strangeness. He wrote not only of lions and elephants, but of horned asses and of dog-headed and double-headed men. The references here are clearly to antelopes and to the masked dancers of Africa.

Africa, so far as its interior is concerned, has always kept its soul untouched. The continent possesses its skyscrapers, its roofs of corrugated iron, its highways, traffic police and airports. Its broad interior, however, and the essential character of its vast landscapes—these things are still part of "Darkest Africa." And that is just what is so odd about it. North America, discovered four centuries ago, is "White Man's Country" today. The aboriginal Indian has largely vanished into the pages of books. Fifteen white generations have transformed this territory, which is hardly smaller than Africa itself, into the continent of technology, the continent that shoots unmanned laboratories into space.

In parts of Africa men and women are still cleaning out irrigation channels with their hands and grinding their corn with a hand-mill. What has happened in the two and a half millennia that have elapsed since the days of Herodotus? What has happened to the process of development we might have expected?

Africa wears armour. When her visor is opened, the stranger looks into the hard face of the desert. Mountains surround the continental colossus, which is formed in the shape of a basin of vast proportions. The edges of the huge depressions, above all Kalahari and the Congo, rise up defensively and then fall away in steps towards the sea.

The rivers force their way through narrow valleys to discharge themselves into the ocean. Their waters rush over rapids and waterfalls towards the river mouths. These river mouths are the exits for the waters of the continent, but they offered no entry for colonizing fleets.

Mountains that edge these vast areas, gorges through which rush the rivers as they near the end of their course, and waterfalls such as the Livingstone Falls in the Congo—these form the continent's articulate geopolitical language. Where, like the Niger and the Nile, rivers flow through great stretches of flat country, deltas are formed, raising up sandbanks against foreign ships. No wonder that, though explorers continued eagerly to feel their way round this part of the continent, they probed the interior only at a later stage.

The writings of Herodotus contributed substantially to the crippling of African exploration. He could see only the gruesome character of the desert; he could see in it only the complete and utter death of the landscape. For him the Sahara was without water, without plants, without human or animal life. This horrific vision, which ruled out the concept of any biological "nevertheless," created for many people a psychological barrier to the interior of the African continent. Explorers avoided this great chamber of death and so failed to penetrate towards the South. It must also be borne in mind that the peoples of antiquity had a peasant conception of life, and that to them the all-important thing was the possibility of cultivation.

The threatening unknown was peopled with spectral figures. The desert itself gave substance to the mysterious notion that men conceived of it. There lurked the fantastical creatures of medieval imagination. The desert became a madhouse of the spirit. Thus the black continent was cut off from Europe not by the sea but by the Sahara.

And so the great seekers tentatively felt their way around the hot mass that is Africa. At first they concerned themselves only with the exploration of its coasts, often regarding it as nothing but a tiresome obstacle on the road to the wonders of India. In 450 B.C. the city of Carthage sent out an imposing expedition under Hanno, an expedition consisting of thirty thousand men and women in sixty ships, each ship with fifty oars. They ventured forth into the ocean beyond the Pillars of Hercules and followed the west coast of Africa. Eagerly they built towns and temples. It is a pity that we cannot reconstruct the stages of Hanno's journey. There is something that really touches the heart about the cautious hesitancy displayed by the sailors of Prince Henry the Navigator when, in the fifteenth century, they battled their way from promontory to promontory along Africa's Atlantic coast, for they battled not so much against any physical difficulties as against misconceptions.

On a map of as recent a date as 1824 the Congo is shown as having only half the length that it actually possesses, while the white spaces, representing terra incognita, are still quite remarkably wide. The interior of the continent continued to resist despite the increased determination with which men sought to lay bare its secrets. The Nile, whose upper regions were already being vigorously assailed in the first half of the last century, continued to guard the secret of its source. It was only in the summer of 1858 that J. H. Speke discovered the Victoria Nyanza, the lake in which the White Nile rises.

"The Zambezi is Livingstone's gift to the exploration of Africa"; Stanley, the Bula Matari, the Breaker of Rocks, following the course of his own austere life, steadily traced the Congo River on to the map of Africa. The meeting of the two men who more than any others helped to open up the dark continent; that meeting, so simple and so unpretentious, between David Livingstone and Henry Stanley on the shore of Lake Tanganyika in 1871, has now passed into the world's literature. It was, so to speak, the climax of African exploration, the Grand Finale in the story of that laborious process—a process stretching over two thousand five hundred years—by which the heart of Africa was laid bare. All that was left in the way of unexplored territories during the last decades was a few spots inhabited by Pygmies in the darkest forests of the Congo.

The dark continent shut itself off from the white man with all the means that its geographical structure provided. The fact that it ultimately did succumb to the process of colonization does not detract from the obstinacy of its resistance. Some things that are happening there today, and which indicate a trend towards de-Europeanization, show that this obstinate determination has continued to the present day. Europe, which once sought to dominate Africa, showing much cruelty in the process, mingled with occasional acts of kindness, will certainly have to adjust itself to the role of the tolerant and tolerated neighbour.

Africa is one of the primeval pieces of the earth's crust. The Atlas (or Barbary) territory is admittedly an exception to this. Youth is evident in its sharp relief. The pattern of folded mountains that can be seen in southern Europe stretches forth its southern branch across the Mediterranean into the neighbouring continent. The Atlas Mountains, in their whole structure and in the shape that earth's history has impressed upon them, are therefore alien to the rest of Africa. Along the so-called line of the Sahara, on the southern face of the mountain system, the two parts of Africa, each of a diametrically opposite character, are fused together.

The greater part of the continent is a primitive, resistant mass. Its core, much faulted in the early history of the earth, had at an early stage been worn down to relict mountains. Into these old worn rocks—schists, quartzites, marbles and so forth—crystalline rocks from the interior were intruded. Over great areas of Africa, extensive tabular strata such as sandstone and horizontal schists have been deposited upon this complex base. Since carboniferous times much of the continent has remained above sea level. From an early date it showed in its main features evidence of its having broken away from a greater original unit. From this primary continent—"Gondwanaland"—India, South America, Australia, and other fragments also stem. But Africa is the largest of these.

What the continent then underwent can scarcely be comprehended from the usual human "frog's-eye" view. Over hundreds of millions of years, the great African block, with other fragments, moved across the surface of the globe. It was pushed slowly and steadily from a South Polar location towards the Equator. Scientists are not unanimous about the causes of this movement. But either tension was released by the earth's rotation, and the continent, under the force of the "flight from the Pole," drifted towards the Equator, or it rode on a viscous flow of magma set in train by mighty currents in the "dough" of the earth's interior. But while the continental blocks were moving slowly—the geophysicists believe at a magmatic velocity of up to fifty centimetres a year—one can perceive, looking back into geological time, renewed faulting.

And here the hypothesis of magma flow is to be preferred, as it provides the possibility of more detailed explanations. In the vertical circulation (convection currents) of the magma below the earth's crust there has been a welling up in places (as though two great cylinders rotating together had combined to produce an upward thrust).

The current now raised the earth's crust. It is in this way that great parts of the moving mass of matter were arched upward. Pressures from below of thousands of pounds to the square inch must have thus borne up the dark continent. Its surface was pushed upward and broke asunder. Gashes of vast dimensions opened up through the whole extent of its bulk. The Arabian fragment broke away from the mother block. Fissures, large and small, burst open in the rigid mass. Systems of such clefts divided the whole unwieldy block. Volcanoes rose out of these long-stretched lines of cleavage. In rows and in groups, and as new features, they were superimposed upon the ancient rock. Their fiery torches illuminated the dramatic scenes of earth's history.

At this point the ocean streams into the huge depression between Arabia and Africa, washing large numbers of volcanic islands with its waves. The edges of the Red Sea remain marked by the sides of this fragmented arch of rock. A tributary cleft of generous dimensions runs southward through Abyssinia, heaping up great covering masses of volcanic material. In the Rift Valley and in the Central African Depression there is a series of long-stretched lakes which continues almost playfully in whole chains of tiny sheets of water. In East Africa, the classic country of these clefts, the earth forces up whole hosts of volcanoes from her hot body. It is the mightiest of these fiery fountains that sends the peak of

Kilimanjaro towering 19,000 feet into the skies. It reaches into the regions of cold air and it is these that place the helmet of ice upon its summit—at a point three degrees from the Equator!

In the Central African Rift lie the Virunga Mountains. Their emergence from the earth is to be explained by smaller cracks in the earth's crust which crossed the line of the larger rift. Here, on February 29, 1948, a new crack appeared, some four miles in length, its appearance being accompanied by a powerful seismic shock. A new volcanic impulse startled the country. Bursts of flame lit up the night. Fiery streams poured over the bush and turned all the vegetation into burning torches of straw.

In the Virunga Mountains there stands Nyiragongo, some ten thousand feet in height. Within its crater there boils a lake of liquid lava. You can see a network of cracks glowing almost playfully on its black skin. Everlastingly you can see these glowing bundles of flame as they shoot upward with showers of sparks, "while a great surging sea of liquid fire beats with scarlet waves against the sheer wall of rock that surrounds the crater" (Haroun Tazieff). Here there has been preserved an echo of that great drama of creation in which the continent was given its shape, an echo that has lasted into our own day.

Africa's lively geological past, the extent and number of such upthrusts from below, and the spreading over large areas of what was thus raised towards the surface, brought the riches of the earth out into the light or placed them where they were within the grasp of modern technology. The geological past is the basis of the most recent geographical present.

The magmatic streams of the early days of earth's history deposited not only granite but ores in the body of the African rock. The Congo, Katanga and South Africa took on the appearance of a continental treasure chest. This treasure chest was both filled and opened by the processes of earth's history.

For the past eighty years there has been find after find, and the world's richest areas in minerals have been brought into the service of world trade. Copper and cobalt, manganese and tin, iron, lead, cadmium and wolfram, gold and silver, platinum and chromium, asbestos, iridium and osmium—all these have been placed at the disposal of man. And among these treasures there lie great quantities of that material whose dull gleam is symbolic, that substance whose hectic exploitation hurled fear among the peoples but also promised unbounded possibilities of technical triumph.

In the Geological Museum in Brussels, behind thick glass walls, there is a lump of rock weighing fifteen kilograms. It is labelled "Uranite from Luiswishi." In Luiswishi, near Lubumbashi (Elizabethville), in February 1913, an African workman found an unusual mineral in the territory of the Union Minière du Haut-Katanga. Analysis showed that it had a high content of uranium oxide. In this glass case in a Brussels Museum that historic moment is held fast, the moment which, though this was unknown at the time, ushered in a technical revolution of the most far-reaching character and what was indeed a new age in human history.

In 1915 a similar find was made on Kassalo Hill near Shinkolobwe, about twelve miles from Jadotville: again there was found uranium ore of unusually high radioactive content. Further exploitation was delayed, for the enormous consumption of munitions in the first world war called for the feverish mining of copper. Yet by December 5, 1921, matters had advanced sufficiently for the first consignment of uranium ore to be shipped out and carried to Antwerp. In December 1922 the first gram of radium was obtained from twelve tons of pitchblende in the plant of the Société Métallurgique de Hoboken in Oolen. Though uranium was first used for the production of radium preparations intended for medical purposes, it nevertheless during the Second World War became an instrument of military and political power by which entire continents were capable of being affected.

In South Africa, thanks to the fact that the soil was only loosely covered with vegetation, the most valuable mineral deposits were easy to discover. The mine shafts thrust ever deeper, and down to six thousand feet below the surface, after the gold of Witwatersrand, near Johannesburg.

In this case a curious helpfulness on the part of nature made work at such depths much easier than it would otherwise have been. The temperature here, instead of rising by one degree Centigrade for every 33 metres of depth, rises by this amount for every 130 metres. At Witwatersrand the warm continent surprisingly provides coolness within its body of rock. Daily some three hundred thousand workmen break out eighteen thousand carloads of ore from which the gold is extracted. Since 1885 one third of all the world's demand for gold has been supplied from this source. Here, then, the collision between black and white, between a form of life that is still very close to nature and the sophistications of technology, is particularly sharp and has very far-reaching effects; frugality and the habit of centuries are alarmingly confronted by the demands and the planning that issue from offices in the skyscrapers. The tension between races and cultures is still far from having been resolved.

More recent volcanic activity of the Cretaceous age had forced up diamonds in steep "pipes" from out of great depths. In the "blue ground," which is the mother rock of the diamond, large concerns in Kimberley are reaching down into seven such volcanic "pipes." Diamonds, both industrial and other, the former coming chiefly from the river gravel of Congo-Kasai, now perform their service to both beauty and industry in all countries of the world. For aeons the dark continent, armoured as she was, guarded the gateway that led to the interior of the earth. Now pioneers of science and discovery have forced an entry, and the most brilliant treasure chamber that man has ever known lies open to mankind.

Tremendous geological forces have thus determined the shape and content of the African continent and have carried it towards the Equator. The Equator, or "equalizer," which cuts the earth into two hemispheres, passes right through the centre of Africa. To this unique position the continent owes other highly individual characteristics and also its grandiose geographical symmetry. The arrangement of the landscape in recognizable belts or bands, each with its distinctive climate—bands that duplicate each other across the Equator as though reflected in a mirror—creates a pattern like the stripes of a zebra. Yet the remarkable thing, the great exciting geographic fact, is that within one broad belt, which under the name of Torrid Zone encircles every schoolroom globe and occupies the greater part of Africa, the most markedly contrasting conditions exist in the closest proximity to one another: maximum and minimum rainfall, the most luxuriant richness of life and the most complete and utter emptiness.

Over the equatorial zone the sun draws air upward and thus initiates circulatory systems that produce important results. Again, convection flows, this time in the atmosphere, help to sketch in the portrait of Africa. The tropical air masses circulate uninterruptedly—ascending fountainlike above the equatorial zone, flowing northward and southward as far as the thirtieth parallels of latitude, descending once more to the earth's surface, and then flowing back to the Equator.

This concept of the two rotating cylinders of air is so simple, so easily grasped, that it might have been superseded: yet even in the most recent specialist literature, in spite of subsidiary systems, it retains its dominant role. The ascending equatorial air precipitates the daily clouds and the afternoon rains. The descending mass, having deposited its moisture over wide areas and being heated by the descent, flows like a scorching oven blast over the land; every cloud melts away, every droplet of water is snatched up. Where this atmospheric rotation occurs over land—and in Africa this is generally the case—then we get the well-known contrast between the hot, humid forest and the burning desert.

The relatively small angular oscillation of the sun's position at the Equator ensures a restricted temperature range. The difference between the warmest and the coldest month at Luluaburg during the course of a year is 0.6 degrees. This means that for all practical purposes there have ceased to be any seasons.

This hothouse air with its constant temperature and its frequent thunderstorms that seem almost to follow a daily timetable conjures tropical rain forests out of the earth, a multiplicity of so-called "green hells." It encourages a luxuriance of animal and vegetable life that has scarcely any limits and at the same time it hinders the human spirit. The Pygmies, culturally the most primitive of African tribes, are still in the hunting-and-foraging stage. Of small stature, and tucked away in the hiding places that the vast primeval forest provides, they may really be a race, dating back to the earliest days of man, which has simply stood still throughout the ages.

In the tropical belts the dry air of the circulating air currents and the scorching sun loose all their cruelty upon the landscape. Together they have torn away its garment of vegetation which in the great rain age of the past covered even the region of the Sahara. The torturing sun beats down from a cloudless sky. In the limpid clarity of the night the earth loses its warmth. In the Sahara one can encounter rock temperatures of seventy degrees and night minima of minus ten. That is why, day in, day out, throughout the millennia there continues a tremendous breaking up of rocks. The residual remains of mountains and bizarre towers of rock bear witness to the overwhelming power of atmospheric processes over the mineral world. Deserts of rock are ground to dust by the merciless action of the temperature. Sandstorms play games with the dunes. They actually cover up entire oases and—a fact receiving constant confirmation—continually extend the Sahara region toward the south.

But it was here in the dry zone, by means of a carefully thought-out use of water —derived either from rivers or from springs—that the world's first example of intensive cultivation originated. Activated by the rhythms of the Nile, the sciences grew up here—as did the pyramids. The advent of the floods was correlated with the course of the stars and necessitated annual measurements of land. Astronomy and geometry made their appearance, as did the arts; these last, which represented an attempt to hold fast what was transitory, carried an African note into the culture of mankind.

The sun crosses the Equator twice a year, ambling in leisurely fashion from one zone of the heavens to another, and in this it is joined not by the astronomical Equator of the globe, but by the Equator of warmth and also by the equatorial rain belt. Thus the territories adjoining the Congo both to the north and to the south—both the Sudan and the Katanga-Rhodesia region, that is to say— receive their summer rains along with the trade winds; these rains are thus like water sprayed through a garden hose that is being regularly swung from side to side. It is a periodic precipitation, one that still necessitates an economic use of water on the part of growers; yet it helps to create an intermediate kingdom between the forests and the desert, namely the savanna.

Innumerable forms of animal life and vast herds have their place in this great landscape and are obedient to the yearly rhythms of the sun. It was inevitable that a pastoral culture should develop in this particular world, which in its turn must also be regarded as an intermediate stage in human culture. The manner of settlement of the numerous pastoral tribes, their possessions, customs and mental world, are all adapted to the physical basis of their lives.

That both at its northern and its southern end Africa has regions of subtropical climate enhances its great geographical symmetry. However, this sketch must not pretend that this pattern is too rigidly fixed. Nature plays around with a pattern of her own. The various landscapes branch out into each other and are intertwined. The forests reach out into the bush, as they follow the rivers. In the desert depressions, valleys among the dunes and dry wadi beds tempt the plain to enter. Mountain forests follow the edges of rifts.

Often the vegetation is affected by the shape of the ground. Near the foot of Kilimanjaro there are primeval river forests, while toward its summit we get upland plains and finally African edelweiss; ferns gleam far above the clouds. Much as the different landscapes mingle, so the waves of white immigrants have flooded over the black strata and built a culture that adapted itself to the African scene. Their plantations, their cattle ranches, their cities and technical installations—these things constitute a new stratum, still in process of growth, which is adapting itself to the old soil and to the pattern traced upon it by vegetation and atmosphere.

And here the picture undergoes the phenomenon of change. Will that change, when complete, be a mask imposed upon the country's natural face? The twentieth century is about to overcome completely, by means of its technology, the powers of resistance that the continent has till now shown itself to possess. There is still much left that is unchanged and unspoiled, and seekers after solitude contend with one another to enjoy these things, and the African landscapes are still and will always remain so vast that they seem without limits. Desert, plain and forest—all these have somehow the quality of the sea. Their sheer dimensions take hold of anyone who encounters them for the first time and assimilate him. These vast horizons find their literary expression in the phrase "the great soul of Africa."

And this same Africa, split up for millennia into tribes, countries, and ultimately into colonial units, has now grown conscious of itself as a single whole; has awakened to life a second time, this time on the political level. Passionately maintaining what they feel to be a natural right to self-government, driven on by tempestuous impulses which often do not choose too carefully between the creation and the destruction of values—the colonizers were often equally undiscriminating—the peoples of Africa have today entered upon the stage of contemporary global history.

In a shorter time than the white man would have thought possible twenty-five years ago, the Africans have freed themselves from their colonial bonds. History helped them in this, for these things happened at a moment when European self-assurance had grown temporarily weak and when that continent was experiencing a *besoin de grandeur* which expressed itself in the form of a far-reaching readiness to grant independence.

Even as late as the outbreak of the second world war there were in Africa only three independent states: Liberia, the Union of South Africa and Egypt. Africa was palpably a colonial continent. In the white man's world slavery had been overcome and was outlawed; the black continent, however, might almost be said to have remained a single gigantic slave.

The end of the second world war brought revolutionary changes. Between 1945 and 1959, six African states became independent; and the year 1960, with all the force of a mighty breaking wave, wrote itself into history as "The Year of Africa": seventeen states celebrated their independence.

The world is seeking a new order. There is a new system of grouping, and men will not so quickly weary of its newness. Africa's peoples have in some cases attained a freedom for which they are not wholly prepared and are feeling their way through the tangled situation in which traditional forces are wedded to new potentialities. The African states are well aware of the fact, already known to many others, that complete independence might well spell isolation and is an impossibility in the world of today. Some of them have maintained close relations with the powers who had previously exercised sovereignty over them. Above all, there is a striving for internal African unity, a continental unity.

Emil Egli

Northern Africa

In this photographic book the African continent has been arranged in three sections: northern Africa, southern Africa, and the tropical belt in between. We decided on such broad categories, because it would be very difficult to do justice to a more detailed division of Africa's landscape and ethnology. Africa lends itself to division into climatic zones because these have a striking symmetrical arrangement due to the Equator which cuts across the middle of the continent.

By northern Africa we mean the greater part of the northern section of Africa down to the southern edge of the Sahara—a common schoolbook definition. This region includes very different landscapes such as the Atlas Mountains, the Sahara, and the Nile Oasis; and the climate, too, varies considerably from the Mediterranean shore rich in vegetation to the glowing heat of the desert, where maps show the highest temperature in the world.

The presence of man, however, affords each of these sections a certain homogeneity. The north is the world of the so-called white African, principally the Berbers, whom the Phoenicians encountered upon their arrival 3,000 years ago. Most of the Arabs, who streamed into the continent from the 7th century on, stopped at the southern border of the Sahara. "The Land of the Negro" begins below this line.

1   *Roman ruins at Sabratha in Libya.*   This Phoenician settlement, founded c. 1000 B.C., reached its peak as a flourishing port under the Roman Emperor Justinian (A.D. 482–565). All that was left after invasion by the Vandals in the middle of the fifth century, flowered once again under Byzantine rule in the following century. But a hundred years later under Arab domination, the settlement again declined never to recover, and at the beginning of our century, all that remained of the city were only a few elevations in the sand. Since then, excavations have been undertaken, and some of the ruins have been carefully restored; a forum with temples and thermal springs, and a grandiose theatre as well as an amphitheatre situated right on the sea are evidence of the luxurious Roman way of life.

2   *At the Hun Oasis in Libya.*   It is believed that the Mediterranean coastal strip once stretched well over a thousand miles inland. Today the landscape is rapidly becoming desert, and the traveller soon comes upon endless, flat, desolate regions where he has to find his way along poorly marked routes. As with every oasis, tracks left behind in the sand by human feet and camels' hoofs mark the approach to the Jofra Oasis Hun, with its date palms standing far out in the desert.

3   *A well at the Sebha Oasis in Libya.*   Similar constructions are used for drawing water at the oases from Arabia all the way across the Sahara Desert as far as Southern Morocco. Donkeys haul water-filled leather bags from the bottom of the well by pulling on ropes down a slope.

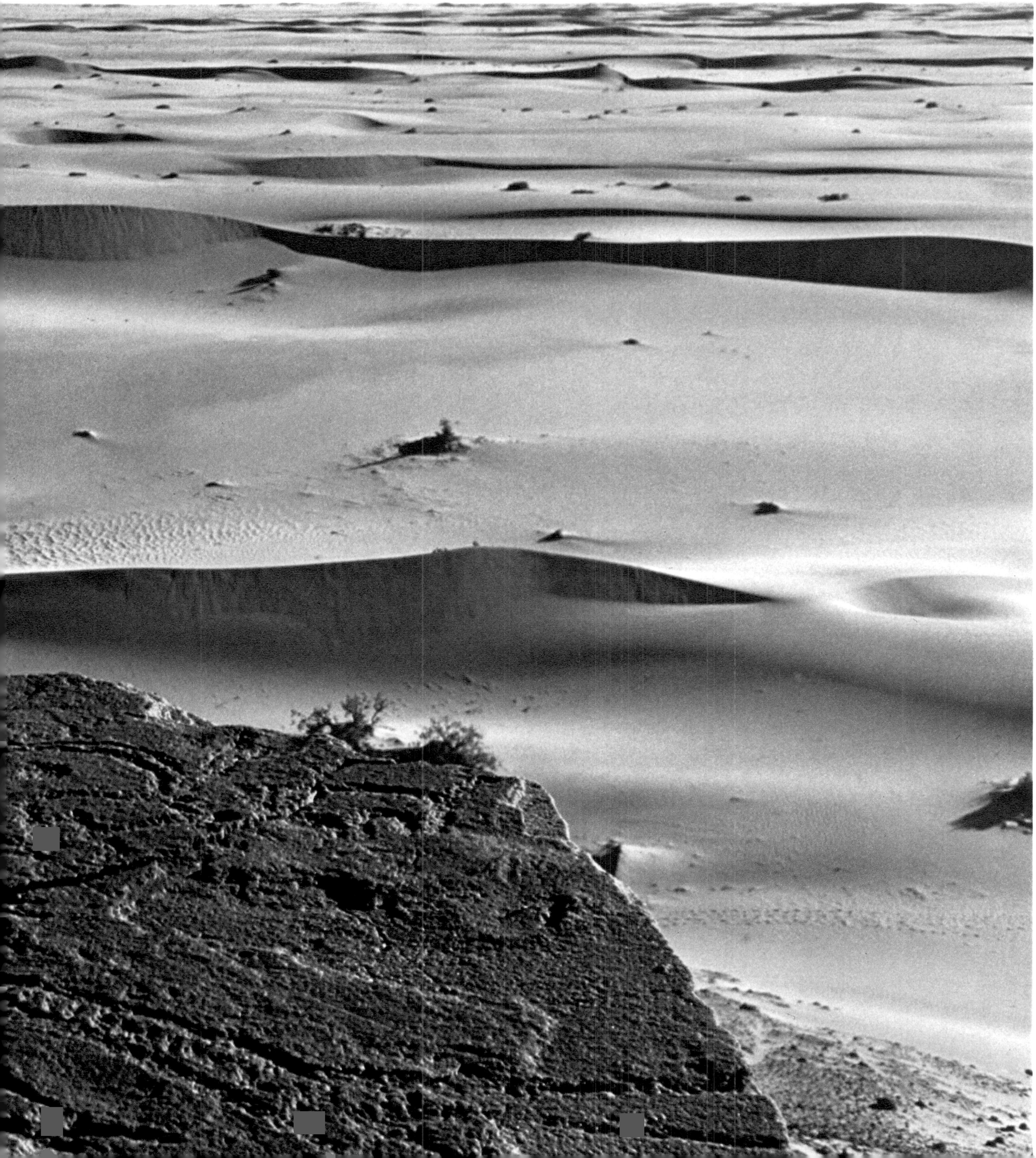

The plantations are irrigated by a system of canals. The man on the left is wearing the small white cap of the Senussi, an Islamic order which comes from Mecca and is especially active in Libya.

4 *A Hamite girl at the Hun Oasis.* The Hamites are a large group of people in North Africa, who speak a language related to Arabic. They claim to be descended from Ham, one of the three sons of Noah.

5 *The Socna Oasis, Libya.* This citadel-like oasis is inhabited by Berbers. Although these people raise cattle and cultivate the fields as in ancient Egypt, they still lead a semi-nomadic life. They are thought to have been the first to begin trading in the Sahara by means of caravans. This naturally resulted in the establishment of permanent market places—a development which originated in the third century B.C.

6 *Sand dunes near the Sebha Oasis in Libya.* The simplest explanation of the formation of the Sahara Desert is lack of rain, due to various climatic phenomena. The annual precipitation never exceeds one inch and vast areas of the desert have less than half this amount of rain. In Arabic, the word *sahara* means both "rocky" and "a great plain." We must therefore revise our concept of the largest desert in the world, of a Sahara in which there are only endless sandy wastes. There are also vast deserts of rock. Even our knowledge of the area can dispel none of its horror. Temperatures as high as 135 °F. have been measured in the shade; but it cools off rapidly at night, so that the temperatures can easily vary as much as 95 °F. in one day.
The older sand dunes shimmer like gold; the more recent ones look white; in both cases, their steep sides always lean into the wind. The dunes do shift, but much more slowly than one would imagine. Those with distinctive features can be identified for many years. The wind gently blows the sand off the tops of the dunes, but it also replenishes the supply of sand. One can, therefore, easily set up camp at the foot of a dune.

7/8 *Drawings on boulders near El Greiribat, Libya.* These prehistoric drawings, on one of the many formations which rise up to a hundred feet above the desert, were scratched into the rock while Europe was still buried under the glaciers of the Ice Age. At the time huge herds of animals grazed in luxuriant vegetation and tribes of hunters tried to improve their luck through the magic of pictures. While Europe lay frozen, life here abounded in profusion. These drawings, of which there are many examples, are not the only proof of a once lush vegetation; an astonishing variety of tools, mallets, and blades from the Stone Age are also to be found. Leo Frobenius has made an extensive study of the most important and most beautiful stone carvings in this area near In Habeter, which are certainly of great importance in the history of civilization. Even today, there is still a controversy as to whether or not these pictures, whose artistic quality has such magnetism, are to be considered works of art. The most widely accepted theory is that they were not created simply for the pleasure of drawing them and looking at them, but that they had a certain magical significance.

9   *On the plateau between Mouridé and Kourizo, Chad.*   These bizarre rock formations are the work of wind and sand. The Kourizo Dunes, situated in the Tropic of Cancer, are considered extremely dangerous; only forty years ago they were still virtually impassable.

10   *Fata Morgana.*   The two horizons can easily be identified in this picture. Between them lies that fateful "lake," which deludes the desert traveller longing for water. The mirage is an optical illusion. The light from the sky and the image of the mountains are refracted in the very hot layers of air above the glowing desert in such a way that they appear as a reflection on the ground. The closer one comes to this "lake," the more it retreats into the distance. But should one stand on the roof of a car, it disappears instantaneously. The Italian name for this mysterious phenomenon comes from the legend of King Arthur, in which King Arthur's stepsister, Morgan le Fay, used mirages to exert her power.

11/13   *Aiguilles de Sisse, Chad.*   Thousands of such basalt rock formations rise a hundred, two hundred, three hundred feet above the Plains of Sisse, which extend from the foothills of the Tibesti Mountains to the Enneri Tao. These rock towers are the remains of what was once a mighty plateau in the mountains. Grotesque forms created by erosion, crumbling pieces of rock, cones, needles, boulders worn smooth by wind and sand: these are the staggering remains of a prehistoric landscape.

12   *The course of the stars over Aiguilles de Sisse, Chad.*   This photograph, which recalls the course of the stars from seven o'clock in the evening until about midnight, was taken at the end of November. The shutter of the camera was, however, also kept open at dusk for a few seconds in order to capture the horizon and the outline of the rock formations against the western sky. In this night exposure, which lasted five hours, the stars look like segments of a circle because of the rotation of the earth. However, only the light from the two brightest stars was able to penetrate the atmosphere closest to the earth.

Antoine de Saint-Exupéry's account of a march across the Sahara, as he describes it in his book, *Wind, Sand, and Stars,* is a memorable tribute to the desert.

"In times past I have loved the Sahara. I have spent nights alone in the path of marauding tribes and have waked up with untroubled mind in the golden emptiness of the desert where the wind like a sea has raised sandwaves upon its surface. Asleep under the wing of my plane I have looked forward with confidence to being rescued next day. But this was not the Sahara! We walked along the slopes of rolling mounds. The ground was sand covered over with a single layer of shining black pebbles. They gleamed like metal scales and all the domes about us shone like coats of mail. We had dropped down into a mineral world and were hemmed in by iron hills.

"When we reached the top of the first crest we saw in the distance another just like it, black and gleaming. As we walked, we scraped the ground with our boots, marking a trail over which to return to the plane... Three days later, when scourged by thirst into abandoning the plane and walking straight on until we dropped in our tracks, it was still eastward that we tramped. More precisely, we walked east-northeast...

"The heat rose and with it came the mirages. But these were still the commonplace kind—sheets of water that materialized and then vanished as we neared them. We decided to cross the valley of sand and climb the highest dome in order to look round the horizon. This was after six hours of march in which, striding along, we must have covered twenty miles.

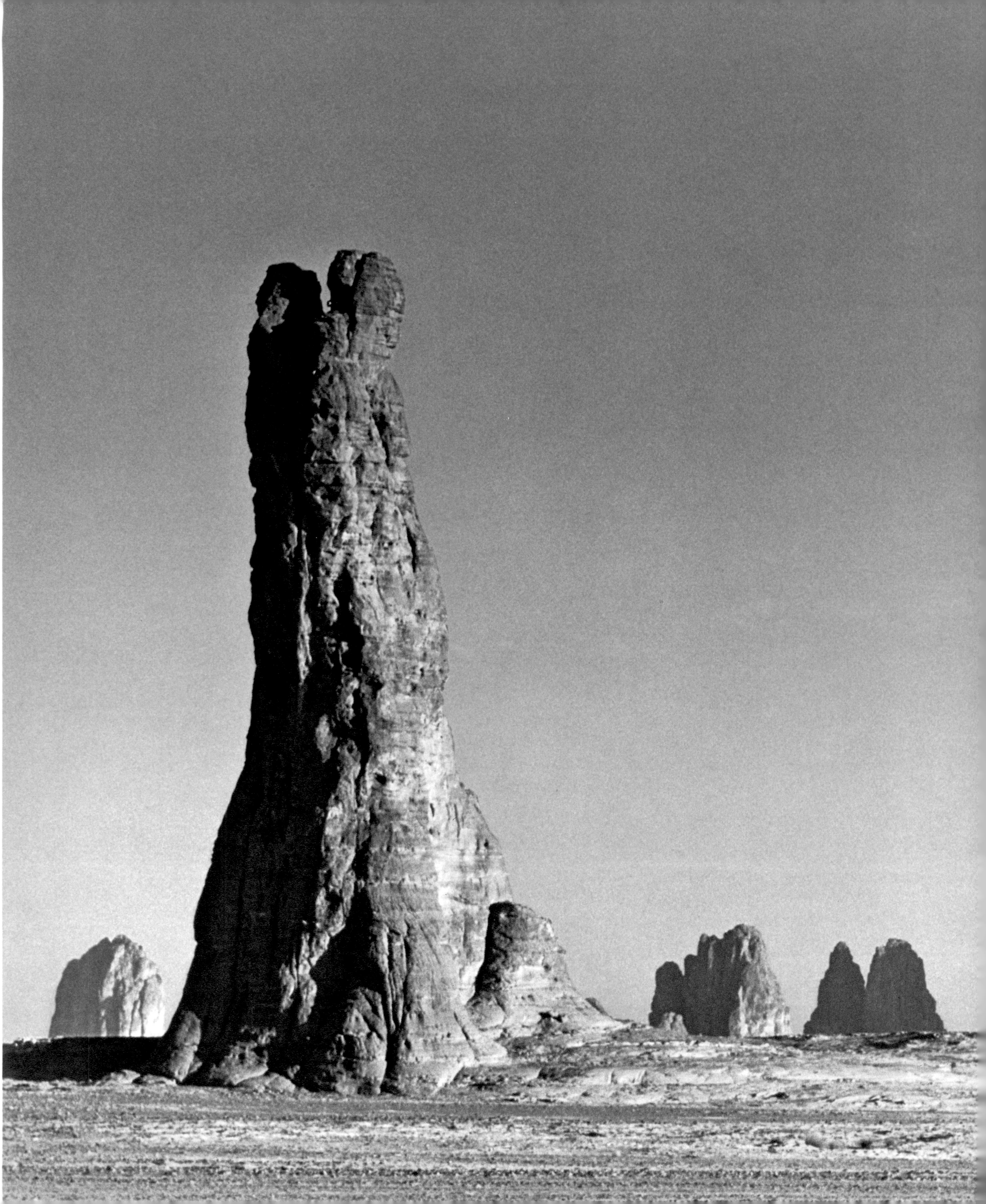

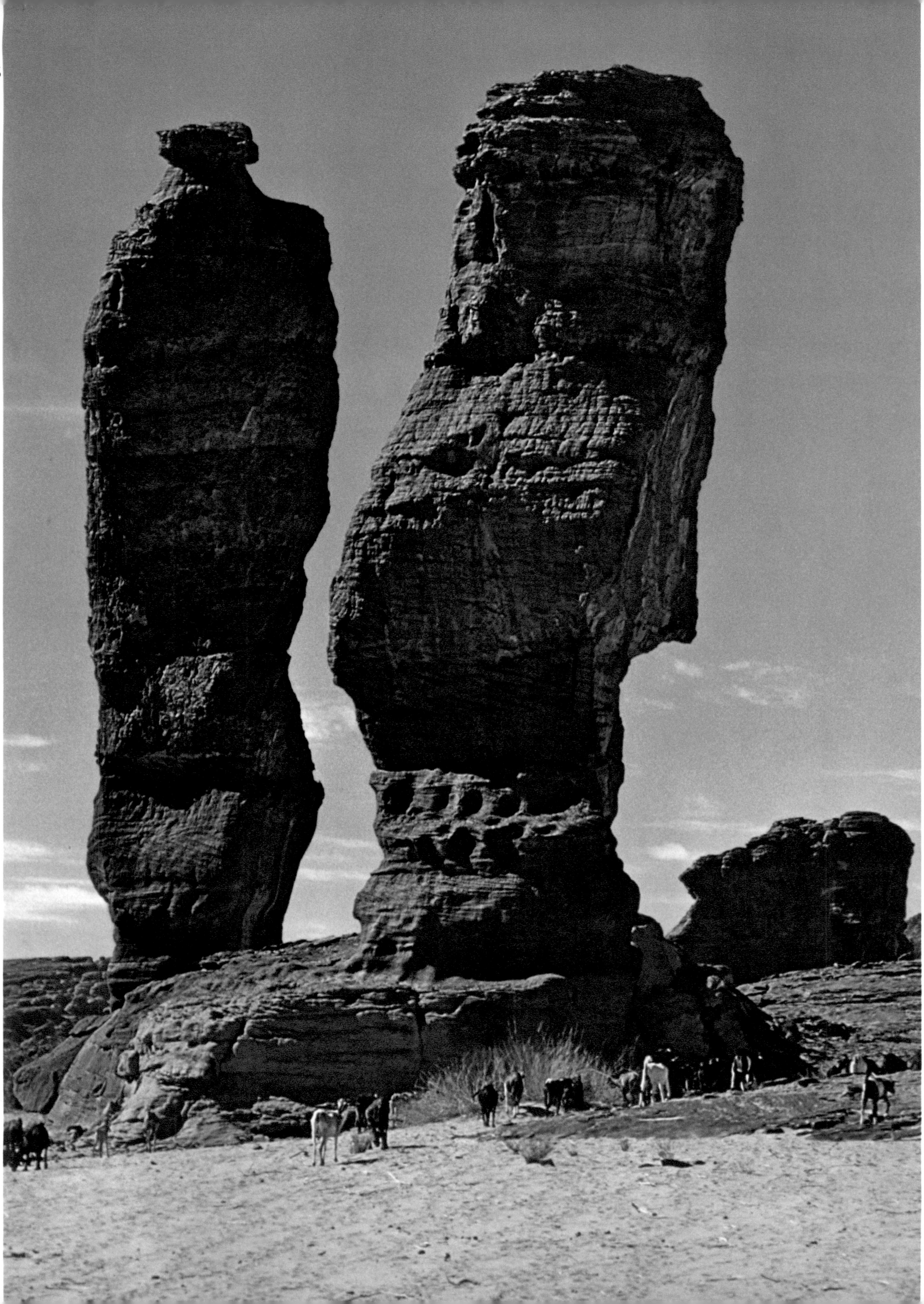

II

"When we had struggled up to the top of the black hump we sat down and looked at each other. At our feet lay our valley of sand opening into a desert of sand whose dazzling brightness seared our eyes. As far as the eye could see lay empty space. But in that space the play of light created mirages which, this time, were of a disturbing kind, fortresses and minarets, angular geometric hulks. I could see also a black mass that pretended to be vegetation, overhung by the last of those clouds that dissolve during the day only to return at night. This mass of vegetation was the shadow of a cumulus…

"I remembered what I knew about the Libyan desert. When, in the Sahara, humidity is still at forty per cent of saturation, it is only eighteen here in Libya. Life here evaporates like vapour. Bedouins, explorers, and colonial officers all tell us that a man may go nineteen hours without water. Thereafter his eyes fill with light, and that marks the beginning of the end. The progress made by thirst is swift and terrible. But this northeast wind was now prolonging our lives. What was the length of the reprieve it would grant us before our eyes began to fill with light? I went forward with the feeling of a man canoeing in mid-ocean…

"I went on, and, finally, the time came when, along with my weariness, something in me began to change. If those were not mirages, I was inventing them.

"'Hi! Hi, there!'

"I shouted and waved my arms, but the man I had seen waving at me turned out to be a black rock. Everything in the desert had grown animate. I stopped to waken a sleeping Bedouin and he turned into the trunk of a black tree. A tree-trunk? Here in the desert? I was amazed and bent over to lift a broken bough. It was solid marble.

"Straightening up I looked round and saw more black marble. An antediluvian forest littered the ground with its broken tree-tops. How many thousand years ago, under what hurricane of the time of Genesis, had this cathedral of wood crumbled in this spot? Countless centuries had rolled these fragments of giant pillars at my feet, polished them like steel, petrified and vitrified them and indued them with the colour of jet.

"I could distinguish the knots in their branches, the twistings of their once living boughs, could count the rings of life in them. This forest had rustled with birds and been filled with music that now was struck by doom and frozen into salt. And all this was hostile to me. Blacker than the chain mail of the hummocks, these solemn derelicts rejected me. What had I, a living man, to do with this incorruptible stone? Perishable as I was, I whose body was to crumble into dust, what place had I in this eternity?

"Since yesterday I had walked nearly fifty miles. This dizziness that I felt came doubtless from my thirst. Or from the sun. It glittered on these hulks until they shone as if smeared with oil. It blazed down on this universal carapace. Sand and fox had no life here, but only a gigantic anvil upon which the sun beat down. I strode across this anvil and at my temples I could feel the hammer-strokes of the sun."

14   *Enneri Oudingeur in Tibesti, Chad.*   Prehistoric drawings scratched into a boulder in the Bardai Valley in the heart of the Tibesti Mountains. *Enneri* also means valley.

15   *A lonely Tubbu wanderer in the Bardai Valley, Tibesti, Chad.*

16   *Enneri Zouarké, Tibesti, Chad.*   The fantastic formations disintegrate in the sandy valley. In the shade of the towering rocks, tufts of grass, gnarled fig trees with wide leaves, and low-growing thorny acacias with leaves no larger than straight pins provide a sparse diet for goats, wild donkeys, and camels. Pigeons and baboons can also be found here.

17 *Wild donkeys in a sandstorm, Erg Bilma, Chad.* The wind whips the sand into a dark curtain, behind which a herd of wild donkeys disappears. Erg is the name given to mountainous tracts of shifting sand, which account for one tenth of the total area of the Sahara. They can be serious obstacles for the traveller, because after a storm the route is often completely buried. When this happens, it is almost impossible to regain a sense of direction and it is even less likely that anyone caught in such circumstances would be found again.

18 *Rock formation in the Enneri Zouarké, Tibesti, Chad.*

19/20 *Prehistoric rock drawings in the valley of Gonoa, Tibesti, Chad.* On the edges of the valley, there are sharp, angular cliffs. Numerous drawings can be found on smooth surfaces and on fragments that have broken off. In these pictures we see a herd of ostriches and a beautifully drawn elephant. According to the chronology of Henri Lhote, the drawing of the elephant would appear to come from the period of the "green Sahara," the so-called Hunter style from 8000 to 6000 B.C. What Leo Frobenius, the well-known explorer of African culture, has said about the rock drawings which he found in Fezzan can also be said of the pictures in Tibesti: "A vast plain of rock fragments, a gallery of rock drawings, lies at the feet of the visitor. Even the very hardest fragments cannot withstand the harshness of the desert climate: searing heat and the sun beating down by day; storms that carry glowing clouds of dust and drive quantities of sand along the ground, slowly and steadily eating away at everything in their wake; icy cold at night. The pictures which once adorned the cliffs and have now been destroyed by the ravages of time and weather can be numbered in hundreds. The fact that these galleries always seem to be situated near places where there is still water today is of decisive significance in investigating the growth and development of the desert on the one hand and the age and characteristics of the rock-painting period on the other. Of equal importance is the fact that the evidence points to considerable changes in the water supply. The situation is apparently always the same: the galleries are cut into vertical walls of rock and facing them is a flat tongue-shaped landscape. Here, in the painting period, people lived, facing the wall of paintings. Stone tools were used at this time and these and the remains of the toolmaking industry lie on the ground. It is from the distribution of these remains that the boundaries of settlements can be accurately determined.

"All the older works must be divided into two groups according to the location of the picture and the nature of the animals depicted. First, there are the wild animals—the elephants, rhinoceros, water buffalo, crocodiles, moufflons, giraffes, and ostriches. These are pictured alone and are always found placed in a prominent position on the rock wall. The contours of the pictures in this group, which is older than the other one, are not so deeply scratched into the rock. On the other hand, not one of the pictures in the second group—domestic animals—can be found in a prominent position on a rock wall. Whether only one animal is depicted or several together—a more common occurrence—these drawings are always relegated to less important areas on the surface of the rock.

"The power of expression of the rock drawings is so distinctive that the basic character of those in Fezzan is unmistakable. Here we find the two North African cultures overlapping. On the one hand, there are the drawings of the large wild animals, of which the oldest examples are lifelike, dynamic, drawn as isolated subjects and not in groups, and given a position of prominence; in fact, corresponding exactly in style with those of Mauretania, in other words, the Sahara Atlas. On the other hand, the style of the drawings of domestic animals in Fezzan has a lot in common with those of Egypt. These pictures originate from the Libyan plains. All

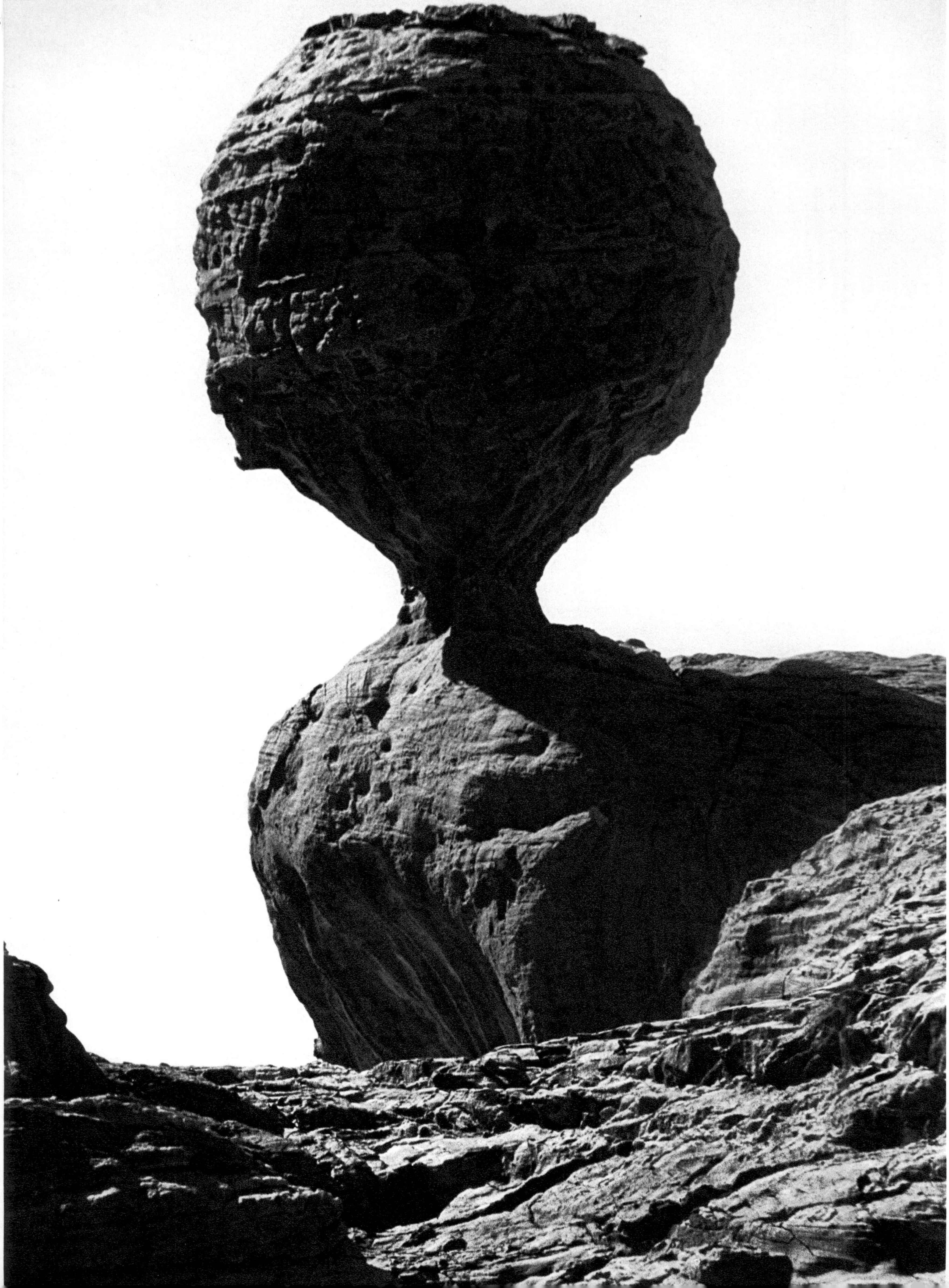

the evidence seems to indicate that these come from an old Libyan culture which, although it had reached up the valleys towards Fezzan, had most influence in ancient Egypt."

The form and movement in the great majority of rock paintings and drawings reveal a familiarity with the animals that only a hunter and shepherd could have possessed. The unique characteristics of each animal and its movements have been strikingly captured. Notice, for example, how accurately the herd of ostriches running has been rendered. The lapidary style in which the elephant is drawn makes it not just any African elephant, but *the* African elephant. The outline of the head and ears, the position of the trunk are "classical."

21   *The Bardai Valley in the heart of the Tibesti Mountains, Chad.*

22/23   *Young Tubbu woman at the Bardai Oasis, Tibesti, Chad.*   There are thirty-two villages in the area where the Tubbus live. The name of the Tubbus comes from *tu* meaning "rock;" the Tubbus therefore are "rock people."

Ethnologically they are a link between the Berber Tuaregs and the Negroes of the Sudan. Although they are not Negroes, many of them are dark-skinned and have negroid features. A mixture of races has been brought about by contact among African peoples due to migration frequently caused by climatic changes, war, the slave-trade, and so on. There is a theory that the Tubbus may be descendants of the fabulous Garamantes, with whom the Roman Legions once had an encounter described by Herodotus.

These two women dressed up in their very colourful Sunday best in order to be photographed. Their finely worked hand-made jewelry and their elaborate hair styles not only reveal a highly developed sense of form but also infinite patience, a characteristic of women the world over when they want to make themselves more beautiful.

24   *Tubbu village in the Bardai Valley, Tibesti, Chad.*   The women in these villages are very shy and make a quick retreat at the approach of strangers. The half-naked children, like the chickens and goats, are not quite as timid. The men are to be found in the villages only when it is time to harvest the dates. After the harvest they set off with their herds and lead a nomadic life on the high plateau, while the women and children remain behind. Their dwellings are always built in the same way: roofs of straw are constructed on a low circular base made of stones. Especially interesting are the oval-shaped enclosures, which serve as a kind of courtyard.

25 *Near Tekro north of Faya Largeau, Chad.*   Rocks rise out of the endless sandy wastes, providing a splendid view of the surrounding area.

26 *Caravans between Ounianga Kebir and Tekro, Chad.*   With great rhythmical swaying strides, the animals make their way across the desert which, like an ocean, stretches as far as the eye can see. The heavily laden beasts of burden are loosely tied together in a long chain; but the mounts, the Méharis, travel singly. These are dromedaries, one-humped camels. Those camels that one may come across wandering at will have become completely domesticated. They originate from Arabia and were brought to the Sahara only two thousand years ago.

27 *Setting of the moon and Venus over Ounianga Kebir, Chad.*   There were ten-minute intervals between exposures. Because it is so close to the equator here—latitude 19° north—the stars sink steeply towards the horizon.

28 *Annular eclipse of the sun near the border between Libya and Chad.*   The five phases are as follows: (1) (photograph in the lower left hand corner) Only two "horns" of the sun can be seen above the horizon. The upper part is covered by the moon. (2) Photograph taken in the 225th second; the sun has retreated still further behind the moon. (3) and (4) Photographs taken in the 446th and 705th seconds; the moon is now directly in front of the sun, the eclipse is circular. (5) Photograph taken in the 945th second; the sun begins to move out from behind the moon again. The ring of the sun visible behind the moon was particularly wide at this point, because on the following day the moon was to be as far away from us as possible. The width of the ring is also greater than it was in reality, because it was necessary to overexpose the film in order to get the disc of the sun.

The "point of the eclipse" is located almost exactly at the half-way mark on the route between Faya Largeau and Kufra, along which General Leclerc's army marched early in 1941. Traces of that famous march can still be found in the desert today. The ideal spot for the photographer is situated at *21° 05′ longitude east* and *latitude 20° 40′ north*. We reached this point on 13th December 1955. Otto Lehmann describes this and the following day in his logbook of the expedition: "13th December.   We have arrived at the spot where the eclipse is to occur according to calculations made years ago, and we are making the necessary preparations for tomorrow. Emil Schulthess wants to work with several cameras simultaneously, in order to get as many exposures as possible during the very few minutes that the eclipse is to be visible. But will everything run smoothly? Have we found—in this pathless desert—the right location on the central course of the eclipse? Will the sun really rise above the horizon tomorrow morning at dawn behind the somewhat smaller disc of the moon, and remain in the sky for a few short minutes —a radiant, glorious ring?

"14th December.   We were already up by four o'clock. The wind began to blow shortly after five, and it is getting stronger and stronger. Because of the storm that is threatening we have to make a barricade out of our jeeps in a great hurry, in order to protect the cameras from the wind. We work frantically; only a few minutes remain before sunrise. Yesterday we focused the lenses of our five cameras on the spot where the sun is expected to appear at 6:05. At the very first ray of sunlight, Emil Schulthess shouts: 'Go!', and Ernst Joos begins to count the seconds out loud: 'One—two—three—four...,' while Marcel Chappot calls out the written instructions: 'Cartridge A—diaphragm setting 16—remove slide—measure light—now— put slide in—put cartridge away—change to Leica 400—diaphragm setting 6—measure light—

now—another one, shorter—now—change to cartridge B—remove slide—measure light—now—put slide in…'

"Then finally the 1125th second. And Marcel Chappot shouts his last order: 'Finished!'

"We are all utterly exhausted; during the last twenty minutes over sixty exposures have been made, demanding extreme concentration, especially on the part of the photographer."

The astronomer, Adolf Lemans, says of these photographs taken on 13th December 1955: "On an average of once every two and a half years it is possible to see a *partial* eclipse of the sun. In Central Europe, for example, partial eclipses were visible in 1961, 1966 and 1968; and will be visible again in 1971 and 1972. In the course of the twentieth century (from 1st January 1900 to 31st December 1999) 226 eclipses of the sun will take place in the whole world, among them 74 total eclipses and 73 annular ones. In Central Europe, however, there has been no *annular* eclipse of the sun as it is pictured here since 9th October 1847, and there will not be another one for the next hundred years. This great variation in frequency is due to the size of the shadow cast by the moon. The *half-shadow* of the moon has a diameter of some 4375 miles on the earth; in other words, it can cover all of Africa. The cone of the deepest shadow, however, is a little shorter than the mean distance between the earth and the moon, so that the earth can come into contact with the cone only near its peak, where it is very narrow. Consequently, the area in which a total or annular eclipse can be observed covers at most a few hundred miles. This shadow glides over the earth's surface so swiftly that only a supersonic jet would be able to follow it.

"It is clear that at the beginning and end of the eclipse the core is only tangent to earth and does not intersect it; therefore the rays of the sun only skim the earth's surface, so that the eclipse occurs at sunrise or at sunset. On 14th December 1955 the first point of contact happened to be located in the Tibesti Mountains and the last near Formosa. The annular eclipse of the sun was visible between these two places in a zone only 217 miles wide stretching across the Indian Ocean and Indochina. But it could only be seen for from 7 to 12 minutes at any given point. To observe such an eclipse, an astronomer would chose a spot in this zone where the sun is high in the sky at a given moment; he wants a picture that is not distorted by atmospheric refraction. Emil Schulthess, on the other hand, was interested in recording the eclipsed sun as it appeared on the horizon; he was not concerned with avoiding distortions. This is why he went on an expedition to find the 'sunrise of an eclipse'—and he is probably the first to have done so."

29/30 *The Oasis of Ounianga Kebir, Chad, northeast of Faya Largeau.* This is undoubtedly one of the most beautiful oases in the Sahara desert. It is situated round a deep blue soda lake. It was here that Leclerc's army halted to rest in 1941. The following is taken from a description of the trek to Kufra: "Starting on 25th January, units set out one after the other for the attack on Kufra. Leaving the palm grove of Largeau, they travelled along a route several miles in width that had been reinforced with palm mats. In spite of these precautions, it was a painstaking beginning: six and a half miles per day. Fortunately, conditions soon improved. The ground became harder, and after the convoy had passed through the dry rockstrewn terrain of Borkou, they came to the plain of Ounianga where they were able to drive along the emergency landing strip on which the few aeroplanes available for reconnaissance were protected against the wind and sand only by some scanty straw mats. At the outpost of Ounianga, the units were reallotted and could have had an excellent rest during the two-day halt, had it not been for the thousand little annoyances caused by food, petrol, equipment, and vehicle repairs."

31 *Faya Largeau Oasis, Chad.*   The fortress in Faya is named after the well-known French general and African explorer Victor-Emmanuel-Etienne Largeau (1867–1916), who conquered and governed Chad under the French flag in 1913. The Tubbu women in Faya carry their large-eyed children under their arms, and baskets woven from palm fibre on their heads. But civilization is unfortunately making inroads here too; the beautifully hand-woven baskets are already being replaced by ugly white and many-coloured enamel bowls.

32 *Camel caravan preparing to leave Faya Largeau, Chad.*   The animals have spent the day resting in the sand under the walls of the fortress. They have now been roused to their feet with great effort, but they continue to resist being harnessed and saddled. Their hoarse cries sound especially harsh to human ears. But this is not the only way camels express their displeasure; they also spit.

33 *Caravans between Ounianga Kebir and Faya Largeau, Chad.*   To reach Kufra the men have to cover 600 miles with their animals. During the thirty days or more required by this journey, the caravan will encounter two, or at most three, wells. That such an undertaking is possible at all is thanks only to the adaptability of the camel.
In all probability, the sight of such caravans will become an increasing rarity. Once, when an American reporter prophesied that the jeep would supplant the camel, a lively leader of a caravan is supposed to have said: "Never! And for three reasons: first, petrol for jeeps costs money; second, there are some stretches of the desert that the jeep cannot possibly traverse; and third, when a jeep dies, you cannot eat it." But nevertheless, the life of the caravans has passed its prime, and one reason for this is the decline of their most profitable trade, the slave-trade.

34 *Mountainous dunes near Faya Largeau, Chad.*   Gently curving shapes; razor-sharp ridges. Endlessly the tiny grains of sand trickle down the ramparts, softly singing, like waves moving in slow motion, the hour glass of eternity.

The German doctor and explorer Gustav Nachtigal (1834–1885) has written a dramatic description of a trek across the desert. Over a hundred years ago, he ventured into the, at that time, completely unexplored desert mountains of Tibesti. His native guides having deserted him, he struggled back across the Sahara towards the Tümmo Mountains, accompanied by his Italian servant, Giuseppe, and five Arabian camel-drivers. The following passage is from his book, *The Sahara and the Sudan*.
"We saw the Tümmo Mountains in the northwest, but they were depressingly far away. Their outline was very faint in the foglike steam that always forms a layer above the desert as the sun gets higher. And to reach the mountains, an agonizing march lasting several days loomed up before us. The sun was mercilessly hot; the stretches of sand between the hills slowed us down terribly. It seemed impossible to reach the Tümmo Mountains; after only a few hours I was so utterly exhausted that I believed death was not far off. At that point—it was still early in the day—Giuseppe and I noticed that our guides and the camels walking in front of us had begun to slow down. This did not suggest the short break that occurs when a camel's load has to be readjusted. Clearly the whole caravan was slowing down. Driven by anxiety, we caught up with the others and our worst fears were confirmed: something serious had happened. The young Tubbu boy's camel was *battâl*, that is, it could no longer carry a load. This was, of course, a terribly painful discovery, but I was in such a bad physical state that I could not

help feeling secretly relieved that already, so early in the day, we had been forced to make a prolonged break...

"We set off again at four o'clock in the afternoon... The boxes had been left behind on the hill; the weak camel was being driven on without baggage, and Bû Zeid's camel was carrying the little water that was left.

"Almost as soon as we had got under way again, I had to exert every ounce of energy to drag myself across the sandy alluvial bed of the broad valley. My knees trembled; my skin, which even under great exertion was usually dry in the thirsty desert air, was covered with sweat. I stumbled on mechanically, in a daze, trying to hold out until the time came for a short rest at night, but I had little hope of success. We had previously agreed that, since our lives were all equally in danger, should someone be unable to continue, we would have to leave him behind—mercilessly.

"At sunset we climbed up on to the edge of the surrounding plateau, strewn with fragments of rock, and suddenly in the twilight we saw that the Tümmo Mountains were apparently much closer than we had assumed. That morning they had seemed to be several days' journey away; now we could see the silhouette of the mountains so clearly and distinctly that we came to the conclusion that they were at most only one day's journey away. I felt a spark of hope, but the conviction that death was near threatened to overwhelm me. Then, in the middle of our barren surroundings, we chanced upon some *hâd,* a thorny fodder plant. The mountains seemed so near and Bû Zeid and the Tubbu boy so desperately wanted to keep their animals alive that they begged that the exhausted and starving animals be allowed to feed on the plant. We let ourselves drop to the earth, the camels ate and, under the influence of hope revived, I was able to fall asleep."

35 *The desert ends and the plain begins, south of Koro Toro, Chad.* North of the settlements lie the notorious drifting dunes of Djurab; to the south the landscape changes abruptly. Coming from the pathless Libyan desert, one suddenly encounters a proper road, the tracks of which cut through the buffalo grass of the plain—and on the horizon, the first crooked trees whose scanty foliage is so impressive after the great journey across the Sahara. The world becomes greener and greener, a vast garden sprawls over the earth, a paradise for animals. Even on the edges of the plain one can come across cheetahs, Ariel antelope, Thompson's gazelle, grey ground squirrels, buzzards, white-necked crows, bustards, huge quail, glossy starlings, bush-partridges, goatsuckers, sparrow hawks, and finches. But at night the tom-tom, the African drum, sounds in the darkness, a magical sign of the presence of man.

Tropical Africa

Specialized maps of Africa show a very distinct change at about the latitude of Lake Chad in the zone of the Sudan. The colours become much stronger on maps showing precipitation and population density, on economic maps and maps showing religious distribution (the clearly defined dividing line between the Mohammedan world and the world of primitive religions is especially striking).

The vast, rugged kingdom of the Sahara with its mercilessly cloudless skies twelve months of the year lies behind us. We pass into a zone with summer rains known as the zenith rains. The earth reacts with enormous vitality to this life-giving element, the bush becomes green and fades again with a seasonal rhythm. Finally, to the south of this moderate zone lies the Congo region with its dense tropical rain forest.

Here is the heart of the real Africa, barricaded behind the great desert, completely removed from all that is European and Mediterranean. Even the kingdom of Allah has been left behind in the desert; we are surrounded by a diversified life and by manifold spirits in this polygenous world.

The highland lakes and tropical mountains of East Africa add a third dimension to the vast African plains. Here eternal snows and icy glaciers force their way into the tropical belt.

36/37 *Massa Negroes between Bongor and Katoa, Chad.* Chad is about twice the size of France. By the mid-fifties the capital city, Fort Lamy, had developed into an urban complex of over 40,000 people; the city had absorbed civilization like a sponge; food was being supplied by air directly from that gastronomic capital, Paris. But just to the south of this city there is an area which is still virgin and untouched. The principal inhabitants here are the Sara Massa tribes, which are broken up into innumerable smaller clans, among which the Musgu are the best-known. These extremely industrious people farm, and raise cattle and horses. Millet, corn, peanuts, cotton, and tobacco are the most important crops; manioc is cultivated in the southern areas near the tropical forest. And, of course, all these tribes engage in hunting and fishing.

In these two photographs we see the so-called "bananas." In the local language *banana* means "good morning" and with their inborn exuberant friendliness the people repeat this wonderful greeting untiringly, so that it has almost become a kind of family name. Carrying sticks, they dance and sing on their way. The men wear loincloths; the women are usually naked, but adorn themselves with necklaces and bracelets.

38 *Harvester from the region of Katoa, Chad.* The mixed racial background is unmistakable in this man's face; it is not difficult, for example, to recognize the Ethiopian influence in his features. And it is thought, today, that these tribes streamed into the Chad region from the upper Nile. Little more than a hundred years ago, people from the Logone and Chari were carried off by the thousand to be sold into slavery.

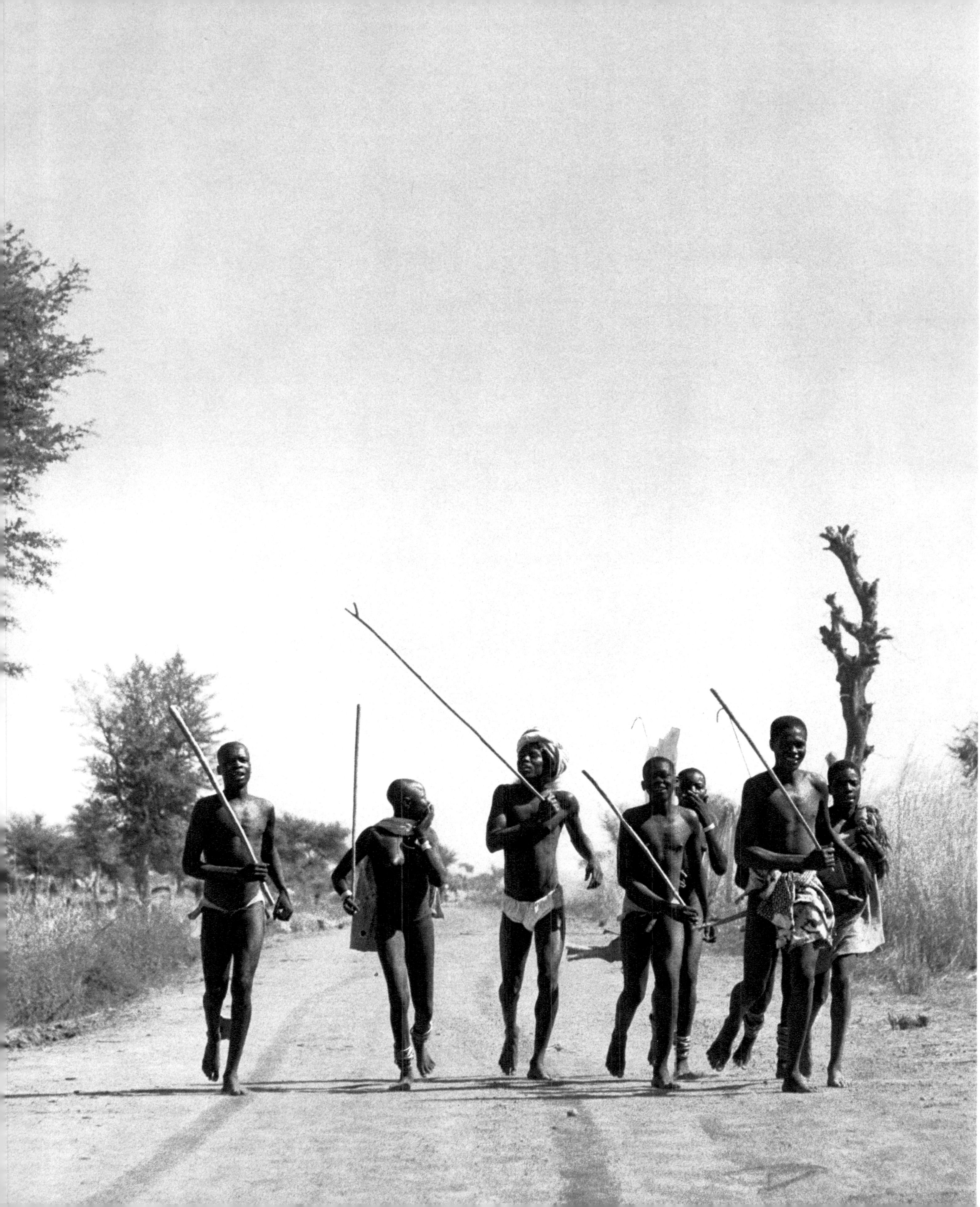

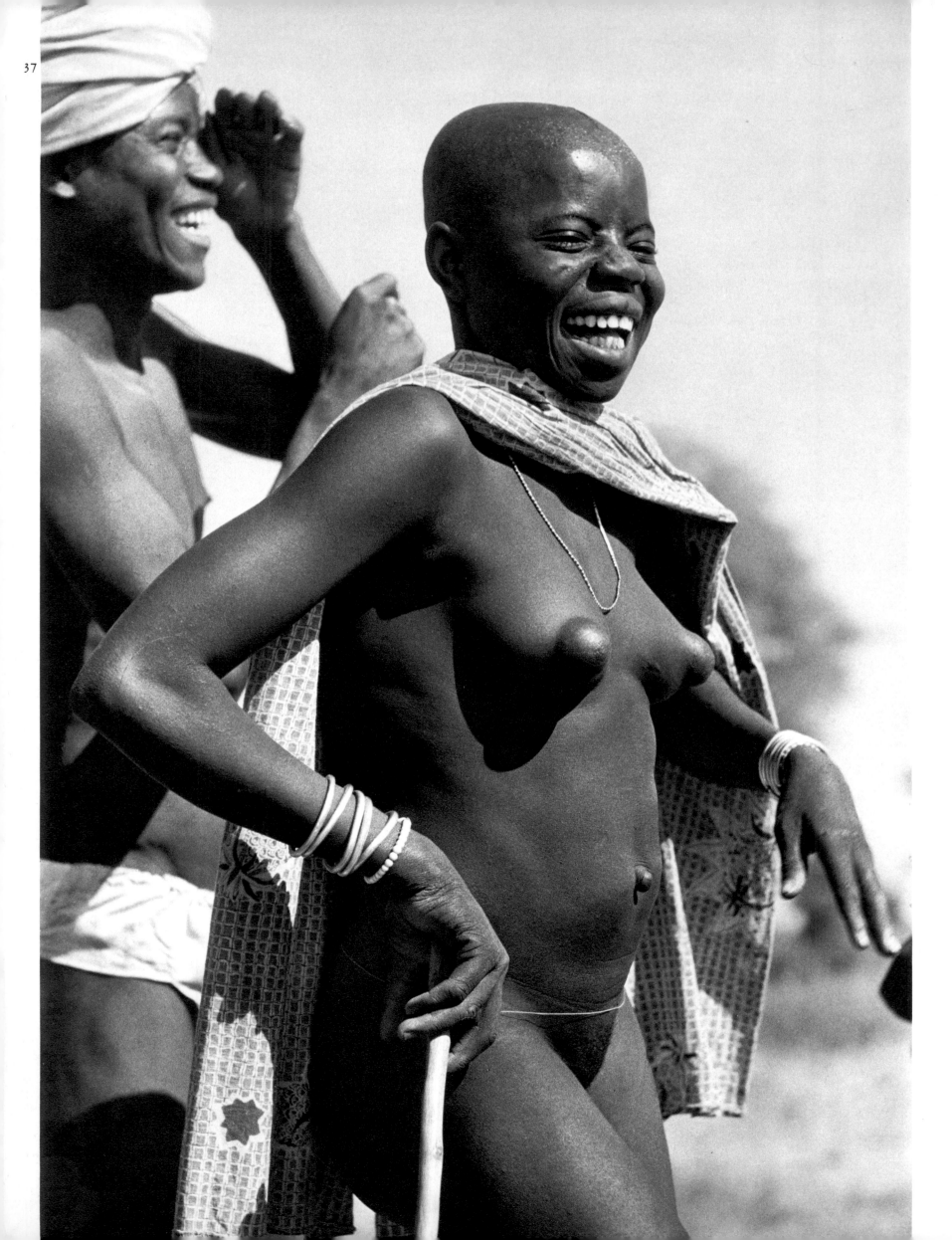

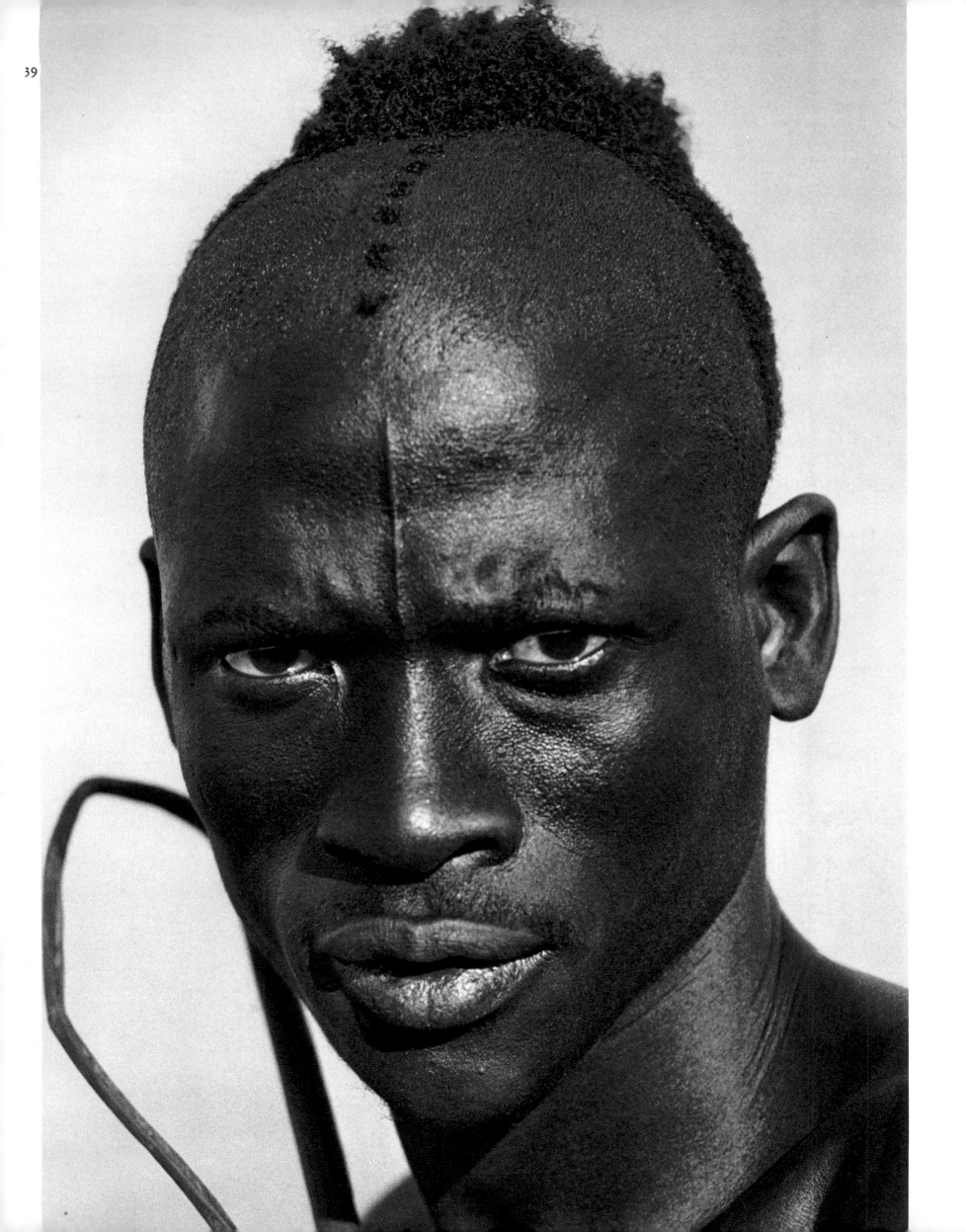

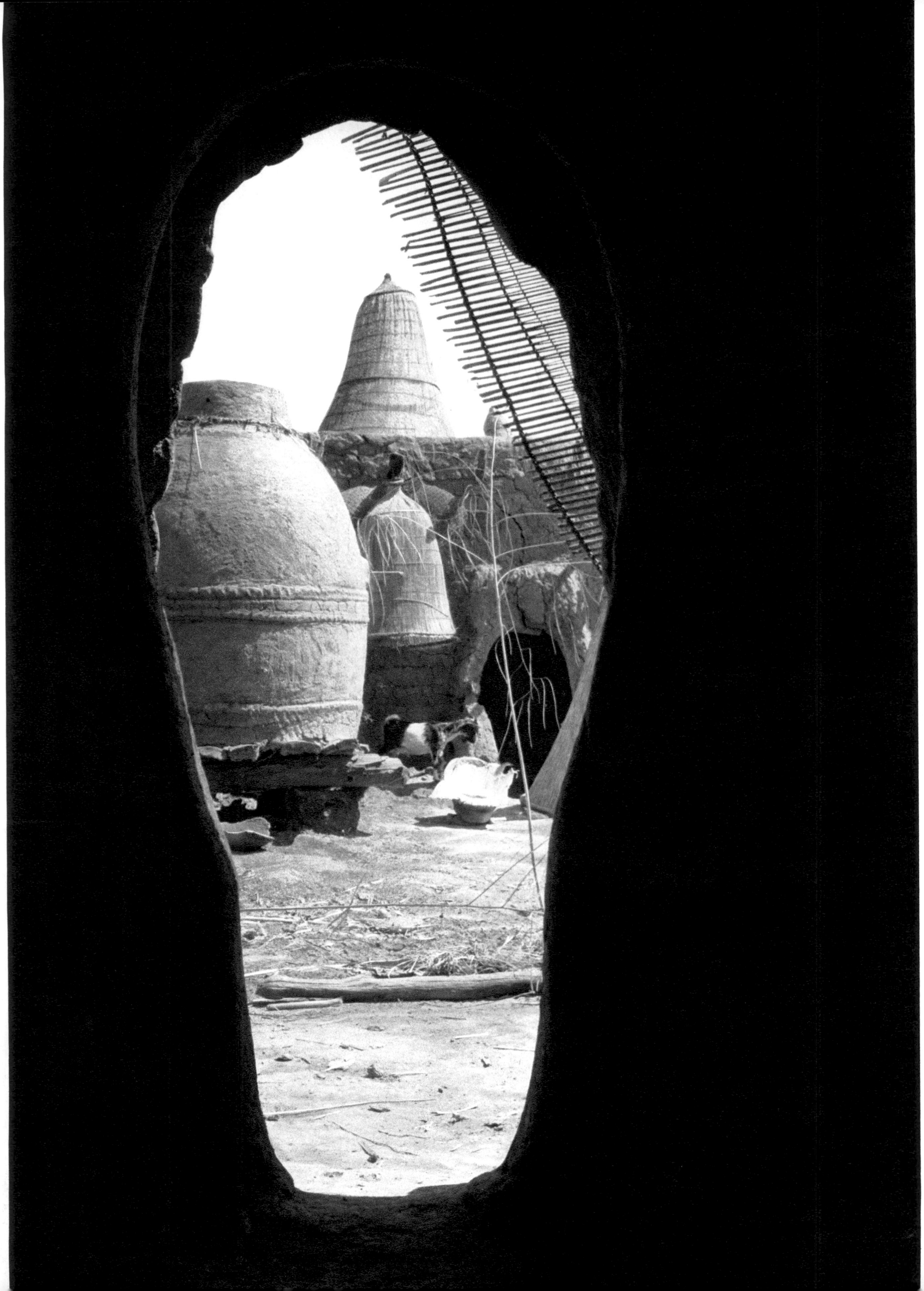

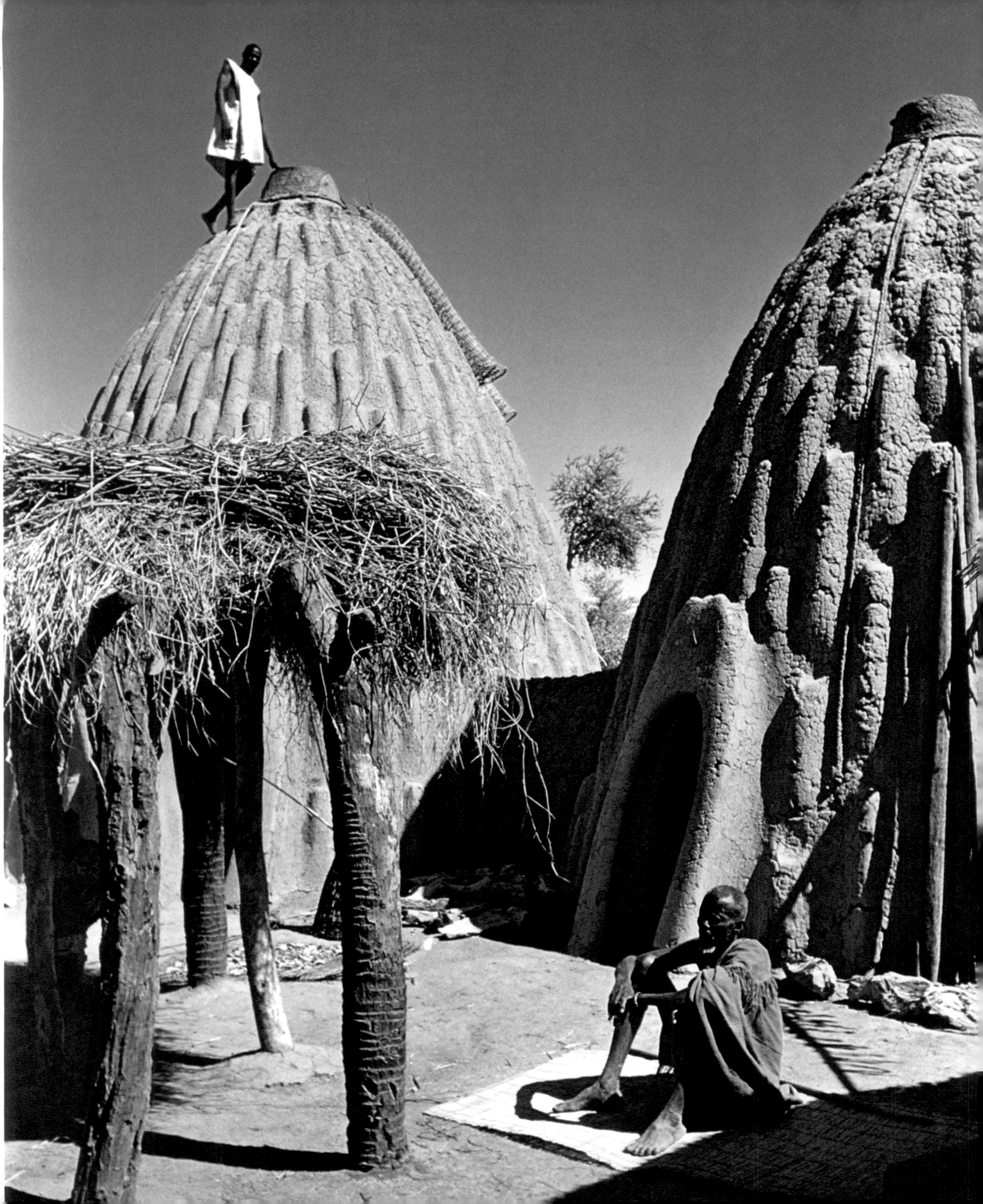

39 *Massa boy, Chad.* These people often shave off all their hair or shave it off in a pattern, and they make vertical scars in their faces by way of decoration. Their territory lies on the Logone, the river that separates Chad from the northern part of the Cameroons.

40 *Massa girls, Chad.* They find themselves water for their morning toilet in a brown puddle near the Logone River—relict of the rainy season. They scoop up this stagnant liquid with their hands, paying little attention to the fact that it is teeming with the larvae of mosquitoes. This process of washing has almost become a ritual and is carried out with utmost devotion. But it also has a social function; it is accompanied by continuous conversation.

41–43 *The clay huts of a Musgu farm near Katoa, Chad.* These houses, shaped like beehives, have in their own way great beauty and perfection. They seem to be built on the basis of the same laws which underlie the artistic construction of certain insects. The clay is not simply piled up to form an awkward-looking hut, but is shaped into what looks like a giant clay pitcher. The houses are meticulously tidy inside. People and animals live together under the same roof. However, they each have a clearly defined space of their own. Above the horseshoe door, which resembles an enormous keyhole, there is something like a very large swallow's nest built into the wall—storage space for all kinds of things. The interior walls, hung with implements for hunting and fishing, are smooth and clean. Lovely pitchers decorated with cord and arrowhead patterns are set out on the ground; this native handicraft is still held in the highest esteem. Here one does not find the enamel bowls and rusty tin cans with which half the world is already disfigured. The fireplace is also expertly built and skilfully decorated with angular and linear designs. The dim room is pleasantly cool during the day. Smoke is drawn out through a round hole in the top of the roof, which can be shut with a lid. The exterior walls are covered with ridges, which are not only decorative, but have an eminently practical purpose: they prevent the rain from wearing away furrows in the clay, and they serve as steps to reach the opening for ventilation. The ridges are sometimes constructed in a herringbone design, but they also often run parallel. A farmstead consists of five, seven, or nine such clay structures built in a circle around a central courtyard. Large pitchers, raised on a wooden platform next to the huts, are used to store wheat and other supplies. There is often a tree in the courtyard where the families gather.

These Musgu farms are a most impressive illustration of the highly developed Negro cultures. They are completely integrated with the landscape, because they are made of native materials, of the straw, grass or clay that come from the plain. The following commentary about "The House of the African" is written by Emil Egli: "All over the world, man's rural dwelling is intimately bound to the landscape, and since the African landscape varies so greatly, the houses also show great variety. Dependence on the earth is revealed in the choice of materials and the way in which man constructs his house to protect himself against the climate. Here, man still builds a nest for himself in the earth. He nestles down close to nature but has at the same time risen above it. Corresponding to the various ways of life and levels of cultural development, dwellings in Africa range over the entire scale of housing, from the simplest, childlike beginnings to the most sophisticated international architectural experiments of today. And since this range is spread out before us as in a museum, we can see how this colourful variety sometimes makes its way into the uniformity of the city. This variety derives from nature's stimulus to the human imagination, while the uniformity of modern housing is the consequence of synthetic building materials, which nevertheless make more standardized building possible.

"The most fundamental purpose of the house is to protect the sleep of man. Witness the hut of the Pygmies—the architectural minimum: merely a curved shield above the resting family. All the other tasks of daily life are performed out in the open: gathering, hunting, preparing food. Nor is the hut large enough to dance in; the house need not be a castle; the jungle itself is an arched roof which slows down the tropical rainstorms. Only the animals and the dripping from the trees have to be warded off.

"But probably the most important building material is clay or mud. The Masai, for example, cover a framework with clay and sometimes with cow-dung; or clods of clay are piled on top of each other to form a wall and are then painted, as is done by the cattle-raising Nakanse people from Ghana. The round hut, simply a circular room with a cone-shaped roof, is very common. In this case the circular walls are usually made by covering a wooden framework with clay, and the roof is made of straw. It is also possible to build an ordinary little house with a gable roof out of the same materials—wood, clay, and straw or rushes—but the round hut is by far the most characteristic structure to be found in Negro villages. The colour of these dwellings, grey-brown or yellowish, depends upon the colour of the clay. The walls in tropical Africa are often a rust-red, because the soil there contains a great deal of laterite. The yellow-brown plains and cultivated fields, the green of thickets of trees, the red of paths and huts, the black people and blue sky with white clouds at noon—all these combine to make an unforgettable composition of man and nature. After a rainstorm, the first ray of sun brings out these colours in all their glory. Should a woman wear clothes at all, she will adorn herself in the brightest colours. Should a wall of clay be painted, then here too there are no signs of timidity or inhibition..."

44   *Fire on the plain near Fort Archambault, Chad.*   The planting season is here again. For centuries the thin layer of arable African earth has been cleansed and fertilized with the ashes of grass fires; so how can the native farmers be expected to know that the heat from these fires also largely destroys the necessary bacteria in the ground? The fire is usually started when the wind rises in the evening, so that it spreads at great speed across vast stretches of land. These walls of fire, fifteen to thirty feet high, are a most imposing sight. The knots of thick grass pop and crackle like machine-gun fire. The noise arouses swarms of grasshoppers, who try to escape from the sea of fire, only to be snapped up with the speed of arrows by hovering hawks, kites, buzzards, and crows. The air is filled with clouds of smoke, and the tropical day is darkened by swirling ash.

45   *House wall with a contemporary painting, south of Fort Archambault, Chad.*   Mother and child of the Mbere sit before the wall of their dwelling on which a picture of an elephant with a human child has been painted. Has the elephant kidnapped the child? Is the painting intended to exorcize such a threat? Is it magic or witchcraft? Or did the artist simply draw an elephant with offspring in human form?

46   *A young Sara girl preparing millet flour, Fort Archambault, Chad.*   Millet, corn, and manioc are the staple ingredients of the diet here. Due to the lack of fat, proteins and vitamins, the natives are susceptible to disease.

47/48   *Cotton harvest near Atanabatagal, Chad.*   Whole villages are employed in the cultivation of cotton. This young girl removes the cotton from an open plant with great care. The beautiful, woven containers bulging with the cotton harvest wait at the collecting station.

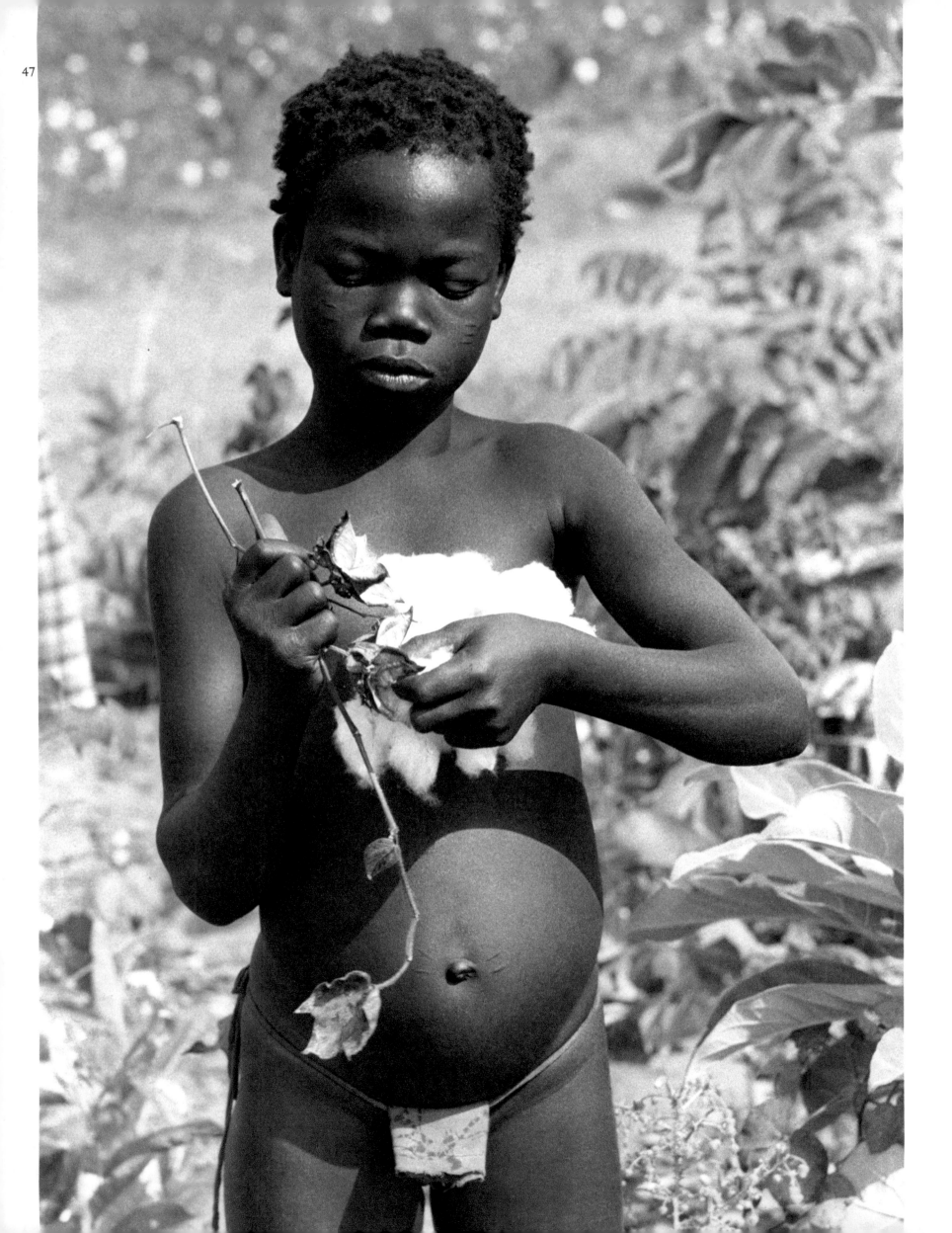

44

Areas with clearly defined rainy and dry seasons are very suitable for the cultivation of cotton, because it requires a great deal of water in the early stages, and dry air in which to ripen. The simple task of picking the cotton has not yet been mechanized successfully, so that it still requires innumerable hands.

49 *African woman with lip plates in Kyabe, Chad.*   Few women here still wear these dreadful ornamental lip plates. There has been much speculation about the origin of the custom, which is fortunately dying out. It is said, for example, that it was introduced in order to prevent the women from being kidnapped by neighbouring tribes. A more likely explanation is that it is simply an extreme form of lip ornamentation, since many tribes insert various decorative objects in holes in their lips. The wooden plates, which can be as much as ten inches in diameter, are pressed hard against the jaws by the stretched lips holding them in place. These women make a gurgling sound when they talk, and saliva runs in a continuous trickle over the lower plate. On her head, this woman is wearing the shell of a calabash into which a pattern has been burnt. The notches around the edges of the ears are also characteristic.

50/51 *The bush near Yanganbi, Congo-Kinshasa.*   Anyone who has experienced the great loneliness of a trek across the desert will recognize that same loneliness upon entering the shadowy primeval forest of the tropics. Man must struggle to endure not only utter lack of vegetation, but also vegetation in excess. In the oppressive hot-house atmosphere of the rank growth of the rain forest, the gentle goddess, Flora, has become a monstrous, power-hungry, domineering witch, who will suffer no higher forms of life to prosper in her domain. Few human beings live in the jungle, and few animals seem able to endure this green perpetual gloom.

Leslie Brown, an expert on Africa, describes the atmosphere in a tropical forest as follows: "The whole feel of a tropical forest is different from a temperate forest, however grand the trees of the latter may be. In temperate forests, broad-leaved or coniferous, the floor is shaded in summer by the leafage overhead. In coniferous forests the shade continues through winter, but a deciduous forest is open, the ground covered by dead leaves. Snow may cover the ground in both. In tropical forests deep shade is permanent, the temperature is always equable and the ground permanently moist. Conditions are ideal for rapid growth.
"On the ground there is actually very little green vegetation. There is a layer of dead leaves, debris, and roots, with some moss and ferns, but this layer rots with surprising speed and is seldom as deep as the leaf mould of a temperate deciduous forest.
"One cannot see far in any direction between the stems of shrubs and the small trees, and the view is further obstructed by dead trunks bearing masses of ferns, moss, and creepers. At eye level there is a mass of shrubby foliage, and to see through it one must bend down. The stems of big creepers festooning the taller trees further obstruct one's passage. In some parts of the forest this shrubbery may be dense, in others relatively open, but it is seldom possible to see more than fifty yards in any direction.
"Above the shrubs are small trees, forty to a hundred feet tall. These may be saplings of forest giants, but often they are species that never grow any bigger. They are known as the understorey, and their chief value is as a nursery for the young of forest giants and as a feeding ground for animals and birds. Sometimes the understorey is so thick that the true canopy can scarcely be seen above it.
"Huge fluted trunks rear out of the understorey. These trunks support the crown or canopy trees, spaced at intervals of twenty to forty yards or more. The flutings of their boles spread into

buttresses that writhe out over the forest floor some distance from the base of each trunk. These buttresses provide support for a massive tree that might otherwise stand insecure, with its permanently leafy crown always exposed to violent gusts of tropical winds. The lower limbs may be six feet thick, and each great trunk soars up a hundred feet or more before branching into a spreading crown.

"Actually this description of three main layers of vegetation is too simplified. In each of the layers there are smaller and larger shrubs, saplings or canopy trees, so that in reality the forest consists of many layers of vegetation.

"Inside such a forest the light is dim and the atmosphere moist, windless and heavy. Far above, the soughing of wind can be heard in the crowns of great trees, but it is not felt among the bushes on the forest floor. The calls of invisible birds, the crash of a falling branch, the yell of a monkey or the shrilling of insects accentuate an impression of brooding silence. One feels inclined to tread carefully and quietly, testing each footstep. The general impression is one of awe. But familiarity will dispel this first feeling of vague apprehension, and to those who know it the rain forest is immensely fascinating and refreshing."

52 *View across the Congo River near Yanganbi, Congo-Kinshasa.* This river carries more water than any other river on the African continent, and is the second in length, exceeded only by the father of all rivers, the Nile. 1875 miles of the total 2735 miles are navigable. The area around Yanganbi abounds in particularly spectacular vegetation. Since the Congo basin has never experienced a geological catastrophe, such as that of the Ice Age in Europe, the incredibly exuberant vegetation has been able to grow rampant for thousands of years. The immense variety of plant-species embraces 3000 different varieties of trees alone, some of which rise to the towering height of 200 feet. Their tops form an almost solid canopy of leaves, and the little light that filters through gives one the impression of being in a tent. The lianas twisted around the trunks are themselves often as big around as a man's arm. The most luxuriant parasites, orchids, and above all ferns can be found growing in the forks.

53 *Wagenia fishermen in the rapids of the Congo River near Kisandji, Congo-Kinshasa.* This kind of fishing demands great daring. During the dry season when the river has subsided a little, huge poles are driven into the river between rocks or in holes especially made for this purpose. The result is a resilient structure of considerable size, which is quite capable of withstanding the racing current. From this scaffolding, large hand-woven conical traps are lowered into the rapids on stretches of creeper. Fearlessly the Wagenias row through the rushing water in long canoes to reach the scaffolding; there they lower themselves into the swirling river to disentangle a fish that is too large to be hoisted up. The women go fishing as well. Groups of five and six at a time wade into the water up to their hips, spread out a circular net, and lower and raise it in a concerted rhythm. It is said that the Wagenias have always defended themselves successfully against tribes that coveted their system of fishing of which they still have a monopoly in this area. Their method of catching fish is so effective that hardly any larger fish are to be found below the rapids; this tribe therefore have the best fish in the Congo River.

54 *Mangbettu courthouse in Okondo, Congo-Kinshasa.* The tall Mangbettu Negroes migrated from the Sudan to the northern regions of the Congo basin after they had been subdued by the Bantu Negroes. In the eighteenth and nineteenth centuries, before the invasion of the white man, they had established extensive Sultanates in the areas where bush and plain met. The Mangbettu people have a highly developed artistic sense, and the paintings with which

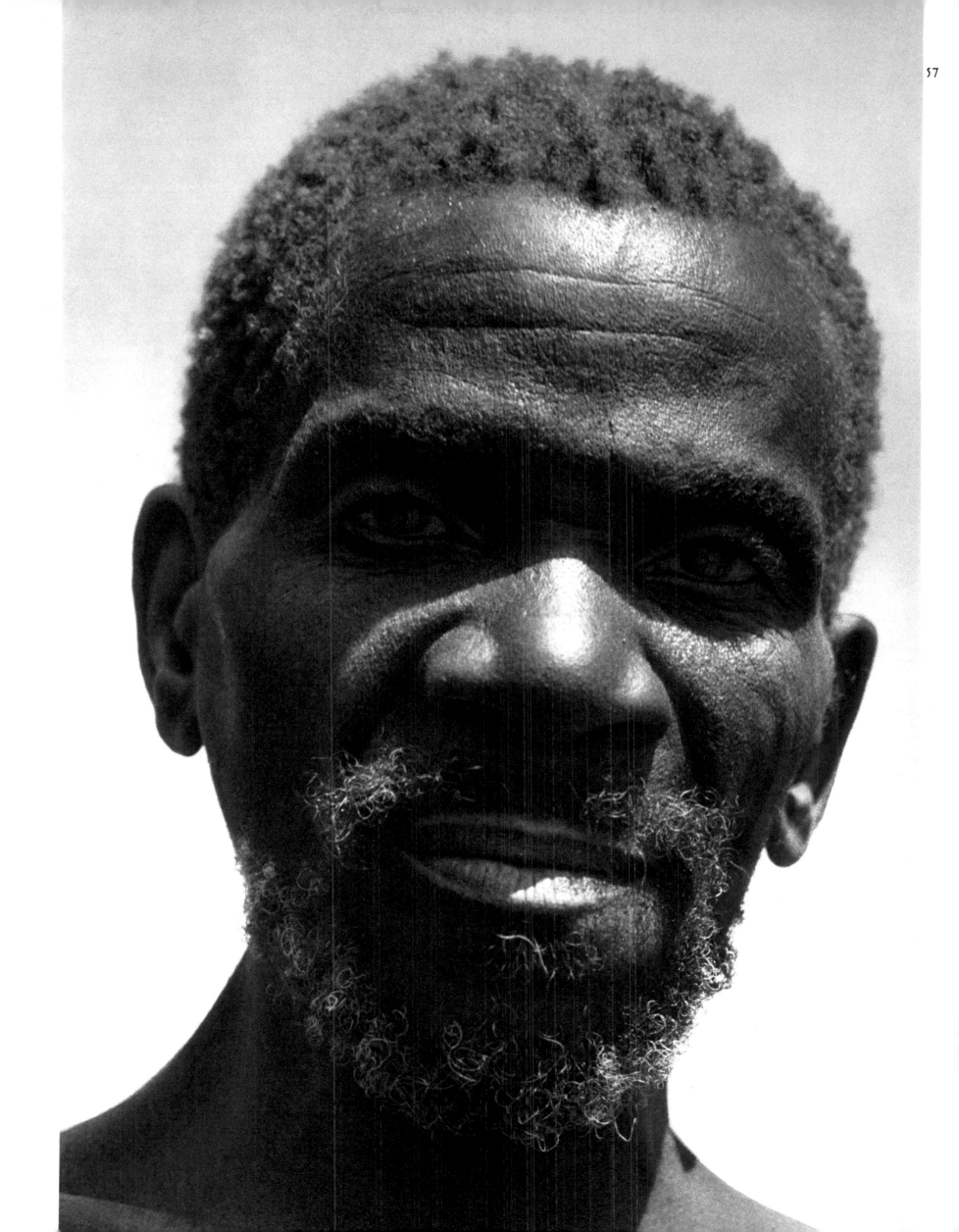

they have decorated their courthouses are most impressive. The geometric designs in black, white, and ochre are especially striking, but the pictures of people, domestic animals and of course wild animals are also drawn with great freedom.

55 *Somali giraffes in Garamba Park, Congo-Kinshasa.* The park consists of gently undulating bush with low scrub and some isolated trees, which are occasionally found growing in small groups. This park, which extends over one and a half million acres, was established in 1938 to protect some of the fauna which is threatened with extinction, especially the square-lipped white rhinoceros, and giraffes such as the beautiful baringo giraffe with its total of five horns. The giraffe's long neck and front legs seem to grow right up into the tree-tops and into the foliage where this herbivorous animal can easily grasp the leaves with its prehensile tongue. Heini Hediger has the following to say from his own observations in Garamba Park: "The giraffe is a walking watchtower from whose behaviour other ungulates often deduce the presence of predatory animals. However, in the Congo these decorative giant periscopes contradict everything one has read and learned about them at school: for miles there is not a single umbrella acacia, which would allow the tallest animal in the world to make use of its height, in the way that is always pictured in nature books. On the contrary, in the Congo these animals are often forced to spread out their legs most uncomfortably in order to reach bushes only three feet high or even the low herbs and grasses with which they must appease their hunger."

56/57 *Pygmies in the Ituri Forest, Congo-Kinshasa.* The Bambuti Pygmies, the dwarfs of the jungle, live in the Ituri Forest which is situated to the west of Bunia. Everyone who meets these people cannot but be impressed by their friendly, open, trusting manner. The well-known African explorer Martin Johnson describes the charm of the Pygmies. He had taken a short flight with a group of Pygmies: "The flight lasted about an hour, and when we landed, we counted the enthusiastic little things as they jumped out of the plane. There were thirty-six, all of whom had flown for the first time; thirty-nine, including us. That's quite a lot for an aeroplane that has a capacity of only ten people." Almost hermetically sealed off from the rest of the world in their thick, overgrown jungle home, the Pygmies are among the most primitive peoples in Equatorial Africa. Their musical instruments, flutes and the *kisanzi*—a little wooden board with strings across the bridge—are eloquent of their retarded culture. The huts consist of a simple framework of poles, which the Bambuti Pygmies cover with banana leaves. Some Pygmies do not know how to make fire and in their huts they have an "everlasting" smouldering wood fire, which they carry with them when they move.

58 *Okapi in the trapping station at Epulu, Congo-Kinshasa.* The okapi is an extremely timid animal, related to the giraffe. Few white men have ever had the privilege of meeting one in the bush; it has, however, long been hunted by the Bambuti. The okapi was officially discovered in 1901, and has only recently become an object of interest and study in the zoos. The demand for it has increased so much that a trapping station has now been set up. The animals reach a height of about five feet and are called *o-a-pi* by the natives who have trapped them in pits for years. At Epulu, which is in the jungle itself, the animals become accustomed to living in captivity (in large enclosures) before they are sent to other parts of the world. Notice the trunk of the giant primeval tree with its prop roots at the bottom of the photograph.

59–63 *A dancing festival in Kiavinionge, Congo-Kinshasa.* Kiavinionge is a fishing village at the northern end of Lake Edward. The round houses are set up in tidy rows; in the middle there is a square for dancing. Upon the arrival of Emil Schulthess, who has been politely called for and accompanied to the dance by the son of the village chieftain, the beat of the tom-toms begins to resound through the air. A great fire flickers and casts ghostly shadows upon the people dancing round it. A young man, whose glistening black body is scantily clothed in a torn white woollen jacket, bends low over his drum and beats it with his fingers. He is lost to the world, almost in a trance, drunk with the rhythm of the beat which has a life and power of its own, although he himself has created it. Every muscle in his body is tensed, his eyes are wide-open, gazing into the distance and seeing nothing.

Soon dancers and singers gather around the drummer. Everyone is there—women, children, even babies. Their colourful calico dresses shimmer in the light, the whites of their eyes flash in their ebony faces. Every stage of involvement can be observed—from blissful rapture to raving ecstasy. The people are beside themselves. Where are they? No man touches woman; no woman touches man. Even the teenagers dance in an island-world of their own, completely isolated; and when some of the dancers, with syncopated steps, circle single file round the wildly beating drum, their bodies still do not touch. Not even the flash of the photographer's bulb can penetrate the heavy curtain of their ecstasy. Every now and then one of the dancers, utterly exhausted and gasping for breath, withdraws from the circle and joins the mass of spectators—only to be gripped again by the feverish beat of the tom-tom which drives him back into the circle. Even the little boys are carried away by the spell, and dance with the same wild ecstasy as the adults. Such a little boy, wearing only a loincloth, bobs among the dancers, gazing into nowhere. His wiry little body twists and turns, his arms and legs swing with the rhythm, his shoulders begin to shake, inarticulate sounds escape from his lips as he moves about among the grown-ups. The drummer has worked himself into a trance, his head is thrown back, his eyes are shut, his lips pressed together. He has become rhythm itself; he is the father and son of rhythm at the same time. A cry! The fire leaps into the air. The dancing slows, the beat of the tom-tom dies away, an echo in the forest; the party is over.

The festivity is over. Surely it was not an end in itself; it must have served some purpose, yet it is fruitless to wonder what that purpose was. Where there are people, there are festivities; even if people have to invent excuses for them. According to Johan Huizinga, a festival is play; it has no real end. "Play may come to an end, but its effect continues; it casts a glow on the ordinary world outside and gives the group involved in the celebration a feeling of security, order, and well-being which lasts until it is again time for this sacred play." Dancing and music belong to play, to the festival; the ancient Chinese say that "music and dance keep the world on the right road and help man to master nature." Such thoughts are not so esoteric as they may appear to be at first glance. It is not so long ago that so-called civilized society felt affronted by the wilder rhythms—whether from Harlem or from Rio—on the dance floor. "Dance is pure play." The significance of this thought is elaborated in the following comment: "Everything that is called music is within the limits of play; and this is true—to a far greater extent—of dance, the twin of music among the arts. Whether it be the sacred or magic dances of primitive peoples, the dances of Greek worship, the dance of King David before the Ark of the Covenant, the dance at a festival; whether it be today or thousands of years ago, here or in deepest Africa, it can be said that dance is play in the fullest sense of the word; that it is, in fact, the purest and most perfect form of play. Of course, the aspect of play does not reach the same perfection of expression in all forms of dance. It is at its most obvious in the round dance and

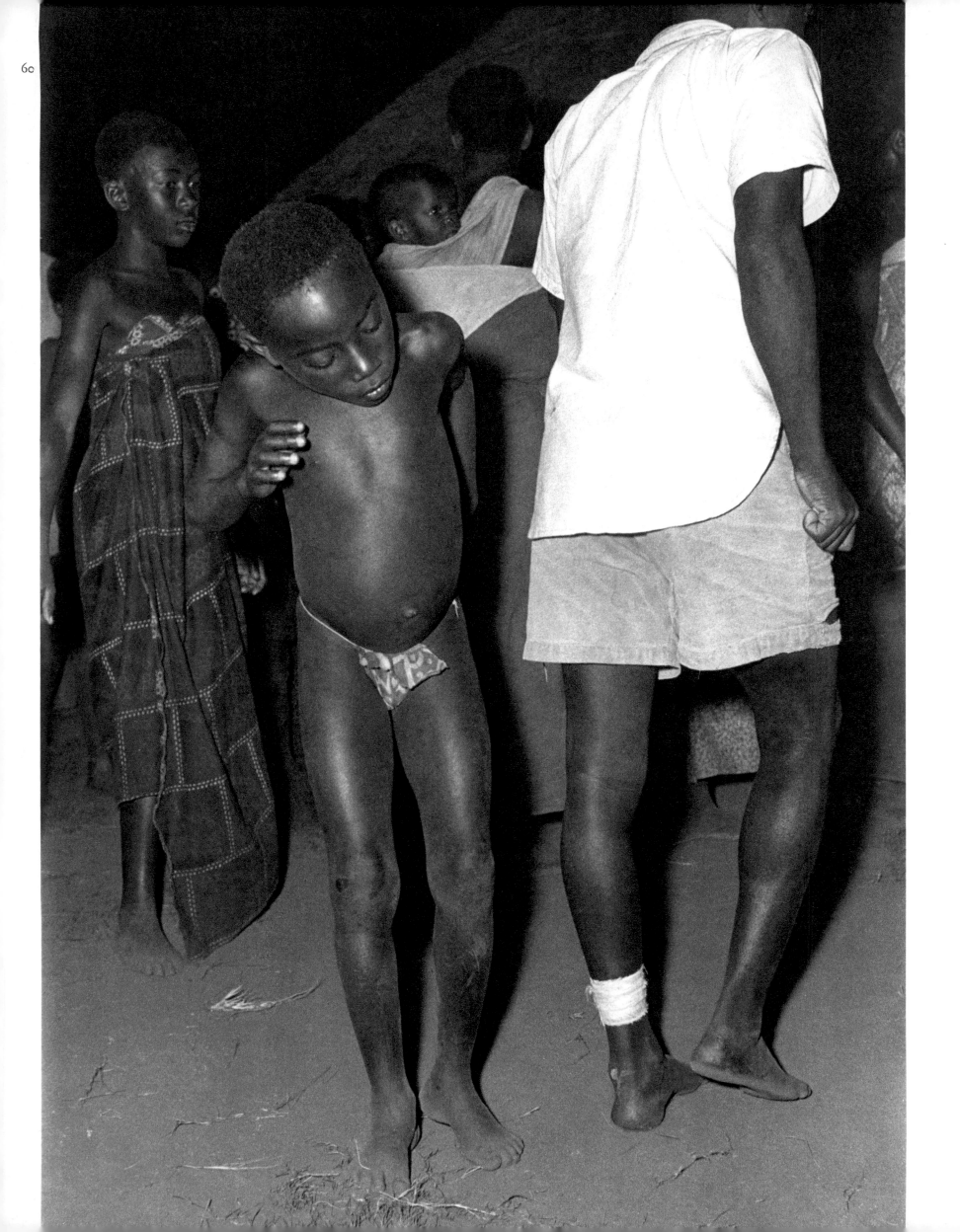

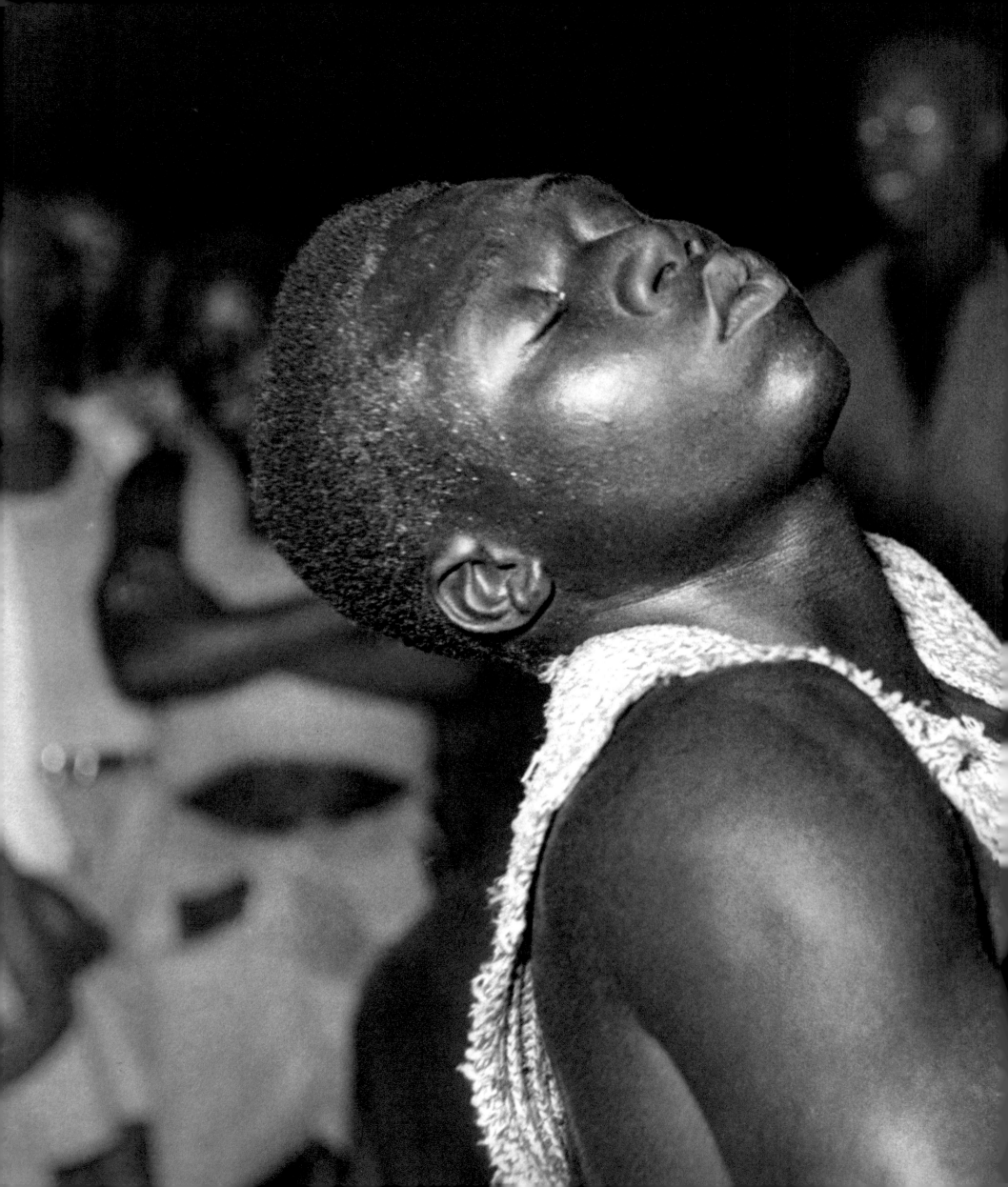

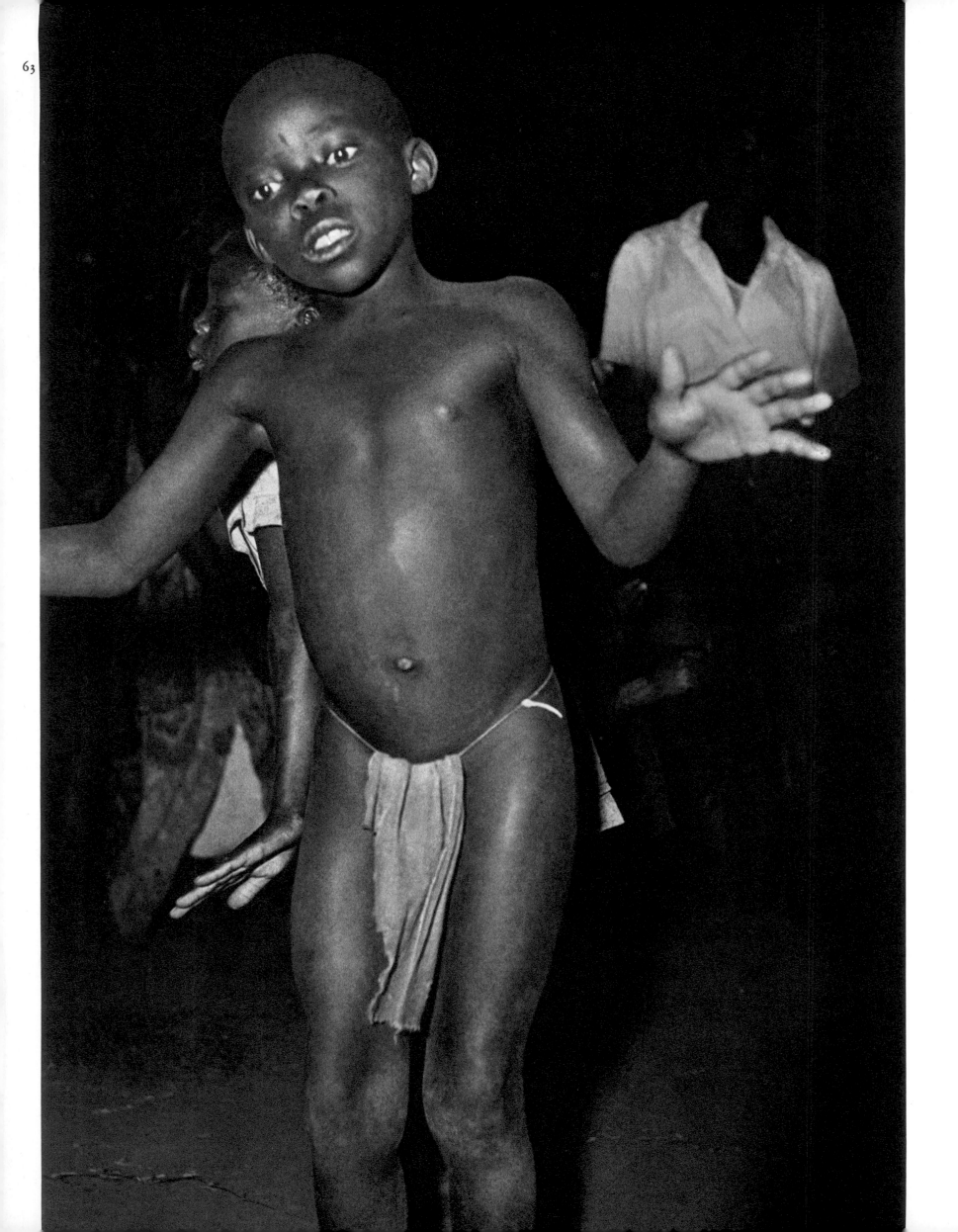

can be observed in the figure dance, and in solo dancing as well. Today the round dance, the line dance and the figure dance are being supplanted by ballroom dancing, the dancing of couples, whose patterns may be circular as in the case of the waltz and the polka, or may consist of pushing and pulling as in the case of the newer dances. Is this an indication that civilization is decadent or impoverished? There is reason to make such a claim; one need only examine the history of the dance—from the heights it has attained in style and beauty to the present day. In any case, it is undeniable that the very soul and essence of dance, the aspect of play, is almost completely lost in the dance forms of today."

64 *The Ruwenzori Mountains on the border between Congo-Kinshasa and Uganda.* The first photograph in the following series was taken in the belt of the Hagenia forest, whose vegetation is typical of the Ruwenzori massif, at altitudes of 6,000 to 10,000 feet above sea level. Glacier ice and luxuriant vegetation are crowded together here within a small area. The mountain climber begins his journey in the tropical forest and the peak which he finally conquers is buried under permanent snow and ice.

The crystalline Ruwenzori massif rises out of the jungle just to the north of the equator. The highest peak, Mt. Margherita (16,790 feet), is the third highest on the African continent, surpassed only by Mounts Kenya and Kilimanjaro. Between Lake Edward to the north and Lake Albert to the south, on the western rim of the Central African depression, the slopes of the glacier-covered Ruwenzori Mountains rise out of the jungle of the Congo to the west and out of the plains of Uganda to the east. The ancient Arabs and Egyptians called this massif the "Mountains of the Moon;" and in the second century B.C. Ptolemy spoke with great insight of "the Mountains of the Moon which feed the source of the Nile with their snows." But the inhabitants of the Semliki Valley call this massif the Rainmaker, "Runssoro," because the area has an average of three hundred days of rain per year.

The "Mountains of the Moon" lay forgotten for centuries, until Henry Morton Stanley once again took note of them—the first white man to do so. On the 24th May 1888 it is recorded that Stanley sighted what he believed to be a blinding white cloud in the glittering glaciers. However, he was not the first to conquer the two peaks, Mt. Margherita and Mt. Alexandra; it was Prince Louis Amadeus of Savoy, accompanied by three mountain guides from Courmayeur, in 1906.

65 *Ruwenzori, 6,800 feet.* The gloriosa, a lilylike climbing plant, shimmers among the delicate greens of the feathery ferns.

66 *Ruwenzori, 9,000 feet.* Tall orchids and dark green ficus.

67 *Ruwenzori, 10,000 feet.* Giant carpets of moss, in which one can sink up to the hips, cover the ground.

68 *Ruwenzori, 13,000 feet.* Near the Kiondo hut (see below for the description of an ascent) senecias rise out of a carpet of immortelles. Their neighbours, the bearded white candles of giant lobelias, grow at altitudes up to 15,000 feet, higher than the summit of the Matterhorn.

69 *Ruwenzori, 16,790 feet, Mt. Margherita,* seen from the Musswa-Messo across the glaciers of the Stanley massif.

The following is taken from the logbook kept by Emil Schulthess and his travelling companion Otto Lehmann of the climb during which these pictures were taken:
"8th February. It took us several days in Mutsora to prepare for our climb up the Ruwenzori Mountains.—Together with Ernst Fröhlich, who had joined us, we set off very early in the morning, after our two dozen carriers had, with great palaver, managed to divide all our equipment among themselves. Their leader, Capita Thomas, began to sing a safari song: 'We are climbing the mountain, will anyone not make it?' And the others reply, '*apana!* No!'—'Will anyone drop his load?'—'*apana!*' they answer in chorus.—'Will everyone hold out?'—

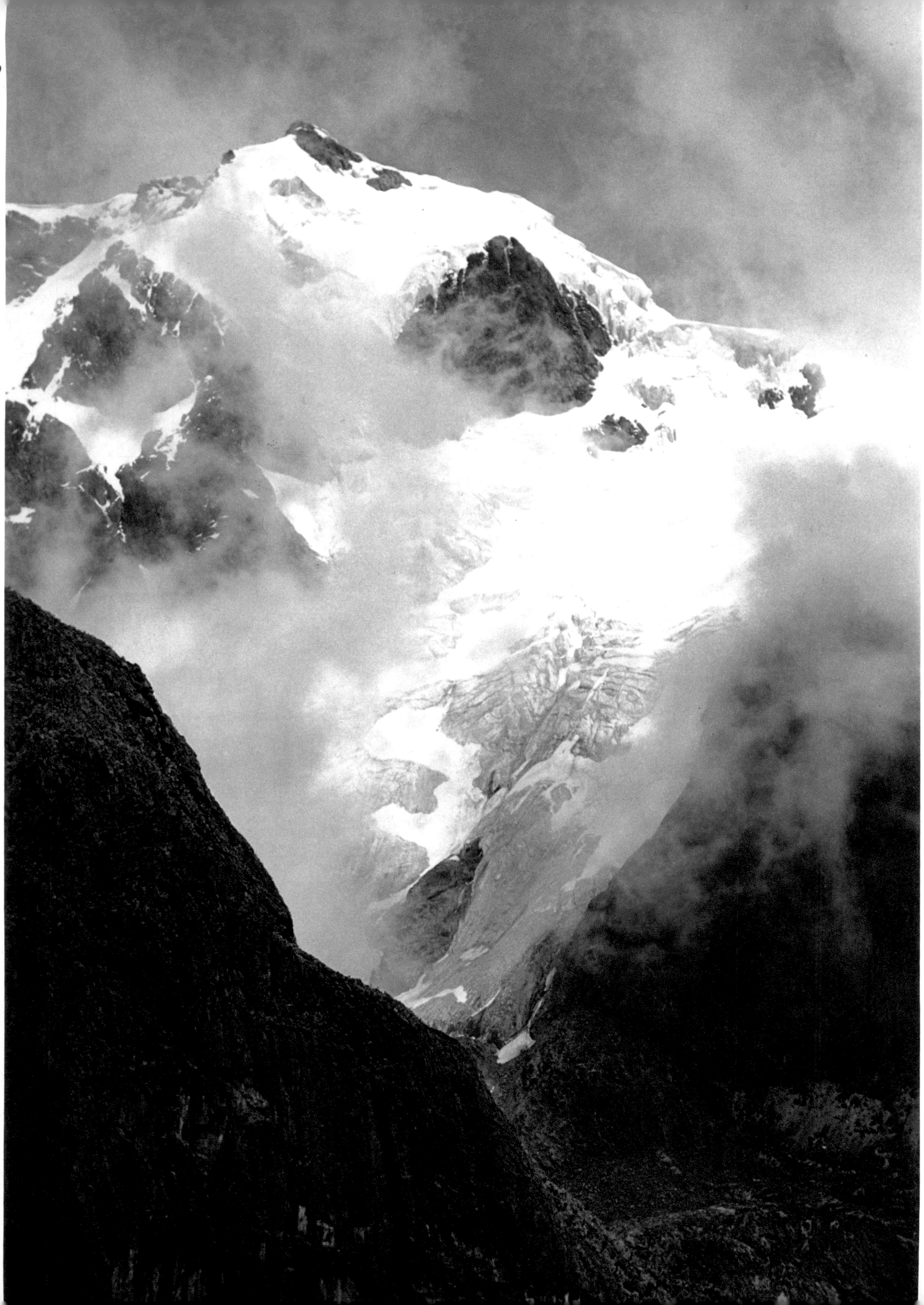

'*ndio!* Yes!' they sing.—At 5,500 feet we reached the forest of the reservation. Below us lay the flat Semliki Valley; the savanna with its high grass and borasus palms; the Butaku River, flanked by small woods and giant mimosaceae; fields of manioc and banana trees and coffee plantations, tiny dark carpets dotting the vast plain; and far off on the horizon the lakes in the mist. We enter the forest; the narrow trail is just wide enough to walk through the green tunnel of lianas, branches and aerial roots. The first stage of our ascent: the Gîte Kalonge, 7,500 feet above sea level. Ferns, three to six feet tall, spread over the ground. Hagenias climb above the relatively low, thick undergrowth. Beard-moss hangs down from the branches wet with rain. Agamas and lizards, and sometimes little grey-green snakes, dart across the trail. Butterflies, yellow, brown, and variegated swallowtails, flit about in the few patches of sunlight that have succeeded in penetrating the thick roof of leaves. Unexpectedly we come upon tree-ferns. It is like being carried back thousands of years to the coal age. The dark trunks with their majestic giant leaf-rosettes rise out of the steaming earth to heights of 25 feet.

"9th February. Shortly after leaving Gîte Kalonge we come upon bamboo. These juicy sweet bamboo shoots—a favourite of gorillas—grow with unbelievable speed, from 30 to 50 centimeters a day, reaching their maximum height of 100 feet in two to three months. One hour's walk later the Erica forest begins. But the heather with which we are familiar has here developed into trees up to 30 feet tall. The beard-moss hangs from the trees like seaweed from a fishing-net. Orchids bloom to our left and right and fuchsias dangle down like clusters of grapes. Giant carpets of moss in which the unwary can sink up to the hips spread out over the ground.—The second stage of our journey lies at 10,500 feet: the Gîte Mohangu.

"10th February. From Mohangu, the trail ascends steeply towards the Kiondo hut.

"11th February. We spent the night in the Kiondo hut. Then we climbed up 650 feet to the green summit of the Musswa-Messo. The view of the rugged Stanley glacier with its jagged cliffs weighted down with icicles and the panorama below—Lac Vert, the forests of senecia and lobelia—is simply overwhelming. We follow the trail upwards towards the east. Soon we catch sight of a precipice, the most difficult spot so far. Even with the wire-netting anchored to the rock, some of our carriers have trouble making their way. Otto descends with them to the Kiondo hut while Ernst and I try to climb higher. We follow the wet, mossy, overgrown trail through a valley abounding in senecias and lobelias. Lac Vert (13,700 feet above sea level) lies to our right. We are surrounded by luxuriant vegetation at an altitude of 13,900 feet. But the moment we leave this steep section of the trail behind, the landscape changes abruptly: grass, trees, and shrubs disappear; an unfamiliar, rocky mountain landscape opens up before us. There is another lake, a smaller one, Lac Gris. It is getting cold. We climb among boulders up a steep step. Unbelievable the way our carriers, supporting our equipment on their heads, tramp barefoot over the jagged rocks and patches of ice and snow. We finally reach the Alpine hut at 14,500 feet above sea level. The carriers deposit their loads, turn round and climb straight back down to Lac Gris to set up their bivouac. Our hut is extremely primitive; the walls are simply wooden planks. It is furnished with a small stove, a completely rusted lamp, and a broom; there are no mattresses, no woollen blankets, no dishes. It is just big enough for us to be able to lie down next to each other in our sleeping-bags. It is getting colder, the wind whistles through the cracks and whirls the fine snow about inside the hut.

"The blizzard subsides in the afternoon. The sun breaks through and, in spite of the fog, we catch blinding white glimpses of Mt. Margherita and Mt. Alexandra..."—Because of bad weather conditions the climb had to be interrupted at 15,700 feet.

70 *Cob-de-Thomas Antelope in Albert National Park, Congo-Kinshasa.* This park covers an area of 2,022,400 acres at the base of the Central African depression, stretches some 180 miles from Lake Kivu almost to Lake Albert, and includes the entire chain of the Virunga volcanoes. A great deal of game is concentrated on the flat, grassy plain between the Rwindi and Rutshuru rivers. "No other area in the world," says Heini Hediger, "has such a wealth of superb antelopes as Central Africa. These graceful ungulates are to be found everywhere, from the gloomy forest to the shimmering plain. They range from the tiny duiker, no larger than a rabbit, to the eland, which weighs as much as a good-sized bull, and they exhibit a variety of horns that never ceases to fascinate. For too long these horns have been collected and coveted as trophies because of their beauty; biologists are just now beginning to inquire into their function, and with surprising results. In addition to the more obvious functions of hitting, thrusting, and tearing, there are also horn formations whose role is more symbolic than it is physical, since they come into play only at certain times during the rutting season, when their use is highly formalized. But it is much more difficult to study the secret ceremonial dances of the impala, for example, than it is to study the mysterious customs of the natives, because animals cannot be won over with baksheesh, glass beads, colourful textiles, or wrist watches. For this reason we are just beginning to study the ceremonial behaviour of antelopes…"

71 *Hippopotamuses on the shores of the Rutshuru river, Albert Park, Congo-Kinshasa.* Countless hippopotamuses live along this river, which flows into Lake Edward. Herds of them numbering from ten to thirty rest during the day, dozing in the water itself or on the shore. The hippopotamus is an amphibious vegetarian, which is probably why the ancient Egyptians called it *p-ehe-mau,* or "water ox." In Hebrew, *behema* means "cattle", and "behemoth" is the name given to the hippopotamus in the Bible: "Behold now behemoth, which I made with thee; he eateth grass as an ox. Lo now, his strength is in his loins, and his force is in the navel of his belly. … Surely the mountains bring him forth food, where all the beasts of the field play. He lieth under the shady trees, in the covert of the reed, and fens. The shady trees cover him with their shadow; the willows of the brook compass him about. Behold, he drinketh up a river, and hasteth not: he trusteth that he can draw up Jordan into his mouth."
The hippopotamus uses its teeth primarily as a weapon to protect its territory from other hippopotamuses. False teeth and piano keys used to be made from the large canines of hard ivory. After the sun goes down, these animals move to their grazing grounds, where they consume surprisingly modest quantities of the scanty grass with their seemingly clumsy jaws. The hippopotamus is left in peace by other animals. Only the calves, which come into the world under water weighing some 85 pounds, must occasionally be protected against preying lions.

72 *Bull elephant near Lake Edward, Albert Park, Congo-Kinshasa.* This animal is a rogue and makes a primeval impression against the backdrop of the forest of Euphorbia. The pelicans make a casual retreat as the giant approaches, but do not let themselves be frightened away. The Congo is the classical habitat of the African elephant, the largest animal living on earth. Efforts have been made here to domesticate the elephant and employ it in the service of man, as is done in India. But all such attempts have failed miserably since the domesticated elephant would sooner or later have had to give way to motorized vehicles, tractors and jeeps.
However, the wild elephanr is of great economic importance. In 1952, Heini Hediger made a study of the situation for what was still then the Belgian Congo, and the results were very disturbing. In that area alone, ten thousand elephants are killed annually, "whereby it is admitted that the number could very well be twenty thousand. Unfortunately, no adequate

substitute has been found for the manufacture of billiard balls, and a substantial percentage of the budget of this colony is dependent upon the export of tons of ivory. In 1946, for example, 273 tons of tusks, valued at over fifty million Belgian francs, were exported. Obviously heavy tusks, weighing from 150 to 225 pounds, which were once available on the market, have all but disappeared today, because the elephants are killed off so rapidly that hardly any very old ones are left. Today an average elephant tusk weighs a mere 65 pounds. Thus the ivory hunter must kill that many more animals in order to obtain a given quantity of ivory. Only very young elephants with tusks weighing up to 12 pounds are legally protected.

"However, elephants are hunted not only for their tusks, but also for their meat. Perhaps the crew of an isolated mine or of a camp for road construction or of a new plantation needs to be supplied with meat. The easiest thing to do is for a native hunter to shoot an elephant, not in the most sportsmanlike fashion. Of course, in a relatively short time, the supply of elephants in the area has been exhausted, and then the next-best thing is cattle, and cattle require land to graze on. This land is taken from the virgin forest; and once the land has been cleared, the loss is irrevocable, because virgin forest never grows up again. Ruthless destruction of this kind has been carried on for centuries wherever there is virgin tropical forest. One cannot but be alarmed by these widespread conditions, and though it is not possible to stem the tide of 'progress', one can at least try to inform one's fellow human beings of the serious consequences involved."

73 *A vervet in a Reclinata palm on the Rutshuru river, Albert Park, Congo-Kinshasa.*

74 *Lion and lioness in Albert Park, Congo-Kinshasa.*   The plain is the lion's natural habitat, where it lives in pairs and even in herds, since it is—in contrast to other cats—a social animal. The famous "king of the beasts" certainly deserves its title; there is no doubt that the lion dominates the animal world on the plain. It preys upon the many graminivorous animals with which it shares the grasslands. Its hunting habits are unique. Members of the cat family usually lie in wait for their prey; lions, on the other hand, engage in a kind of drive. The lion, for example, chases a herd of antelope or a single animal towards the lioness, waiting in ambush, since she is more skilful at pouncing upon the kill. The lion's roar during such a hunt is also unique; other cats cannot roar—they can only spit, caterwaul, miaow, and purr. The lion's favourite prey are wildebeest, almost all species of antelope, young buffalo, and zebras. The last-named, however, are capable of putting up a very strong fight with their hoofs. Giraffes also defend themselves valiantly and are attacked only by several lions together. The tales told about lions would fill books, should one wish to collect them. And these animals really do have characteristics of a heroic and legend-making nature. Perhaps the most apt description of the lion and the role it plays in its environment comes from the Suaheli people, who claim that when a lion roars, it is saying, "Ntschi ja nani? Jangu, jangu, jangu!"—which means "Whose land is this? Mine, mine, mine!"

75 *Cape buffalo on the Rwindi-Rutshuru plain, Albert Park, Congo-Kinshasa.*   It is not unusual to encounter herds of over a hundred animals here. The buffalo is said to be the most dangerous animal on the continent. However, according to Heini Hediger, this is true only of the wounded animal. His opinion is supported by evidence from the epitaphs of buffalo hunters, whose graves are found here and there on the plain, and by statistics from the colonial hospitals. On the other hand, with a single movement of one's arm, it is possible to frighten an entire herd of buffalo into taking sudden flight.

76   *The Nyiragongo volcano, Albert Park, Congo-Kinshasa.*   Heavy clouds envelop the summit of this volcano, which rises out of the plains. The Kivu volcanic area lies 90 miles south of the equator near the border of Uganda. Like a dam this chain of volcanoes, which cuts across the "African depression," collects the waters of Lake Kivu into a vast natural reservoir. The area is rich in marked contrasts. To begin with, these volcanoes situated in the heart of the tropics are often covered with snow. In Kisenyi, on the shores of Lake Kivu, there are colonies of villas, known as the African Riviera; yet only a few miles away elephants roam through the bush. And although the reflection from the fire of the dangerously close volcano glows in the sky at night, the area is densely populated. Eruptions and outpourings of lava are not uncommon. The cities of Goma and Kisenyi, which are quite respectable in size, lie almost directly at the foot of the active Nyiragongo volcano.

77   *View of the upper shelf from the edge of the Nyiragongo crater.*   The actual crater, with its lake of molton lava, lies below this platform. The volcano expert André Meyer accompanied Emil Schulthess from the edge of the crater down to the platform over a 600-foot cliff at an angle of 70 degrees. He makes the following observations: "One is at this point 11,380 feet above sea level and 6,500 feet above the surface of Lake Kivu. Nyirangongo's neighbours, the extinct Mikeno and Karisimbi volcanoes, are still well over 3,000 feet higher and dream of their mighty past, while their younger brother threateningly spews forth smoke. Nyiragongo is the perfect image of a volcano—the way adults imagine it and children draw it. It is a truncated cone out of which white clouds of steam continuously rise up and drift westward. For the scientist, it is the only volcano in the world that still has a permanent lake of molten lava. Almost exactly the same dramatic spectacle lies at the feet of the visitor looking down from the upper edge of the crater as that which opened up before the German explorer Count von Götzen, who in 1894 discovered the Nyiragongo and was the first white man to conquer this mountain. Permission to climb down into the crater is seldom granted, because the descent is so dangerous. The English colonist Burtt was the first human being to succeed in climbing down to the upper platform, in 1930."

78   *Floor of the upper shelf in the Nyiragongo crater.*   "Solidified waves of lava," notes André Meyer, "traverse the surface of the upper shelf, which marks the level once attained by the lava lake. The uneven surface conceals fissures and cavities of considerable depth. The level of the lava lake has receded 6,900 feet, but it is believed that it once reached an elevation of some 13,350 feet, which means that the mountain itself must once have been some 1,650 feet higher before the summit collapsed.
"The crater is a kingdom of pure rock; there is no vegetation whatsoever. The steep walls of the crater are distinguished by layers of grey and brown rock cut across by white bands of rock which wind their way up to the top of the crater. The grey layers are ancient streams of lava, the brown ones are layers of tuff, and the white bands are lava that once flowed into still older crevices and solidified there. Boulders of three cubic feet have broken off the wall of the crater and now lie on the shelf. They contain nephelite and crystals of leucite the size of a fist—the largest known in the world, even bigger than those from Rocca Monfino, in Italy, which are found in many mineral collections."

79/80   *View from the upper shelf into the lava lake of Nyiragongo.*   Spectacular yellow-red fountains of fire spurt into the air, erupting on the surface of the molten lava, which is criss-crossed by hundreds of fiery glowing fissures. As these masses collapse and melt into the lava again, they

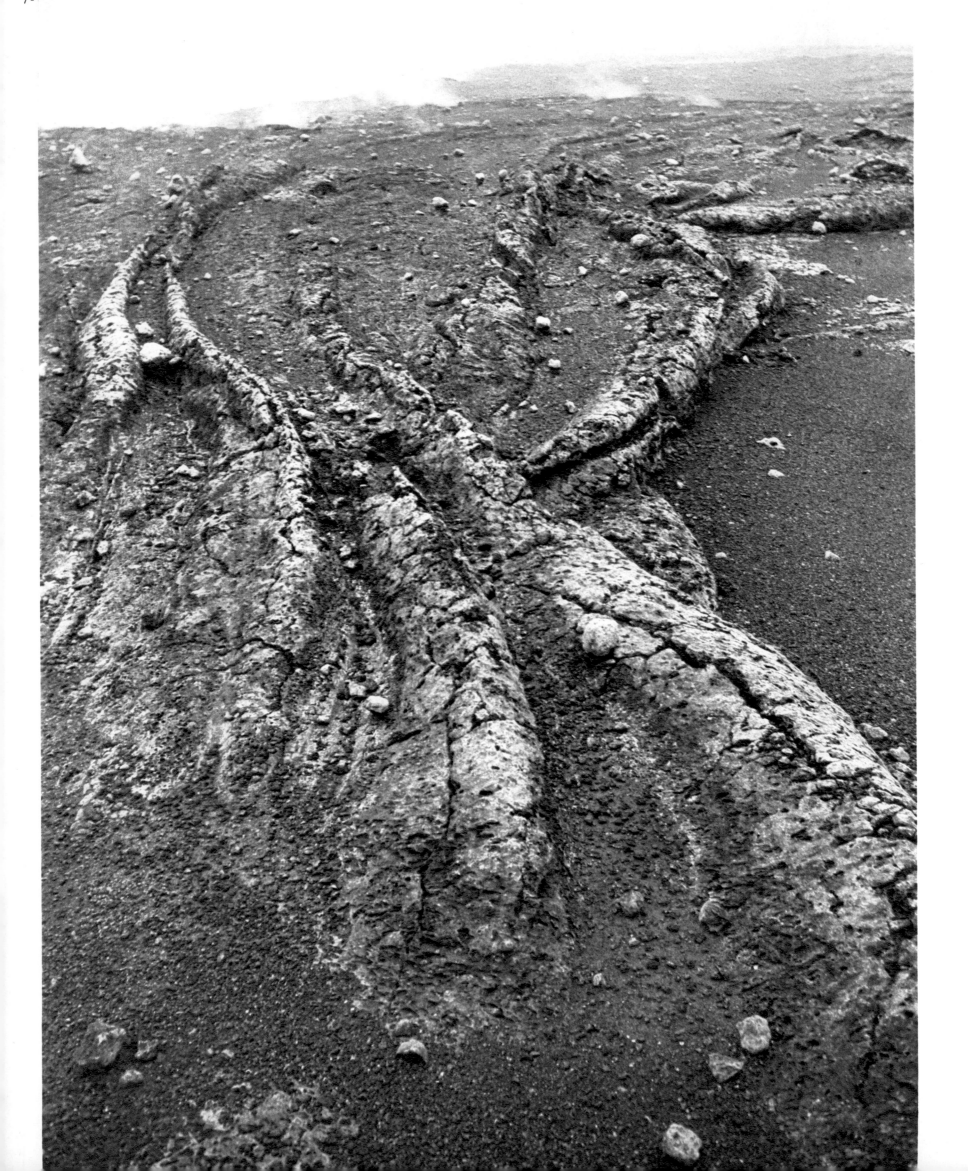

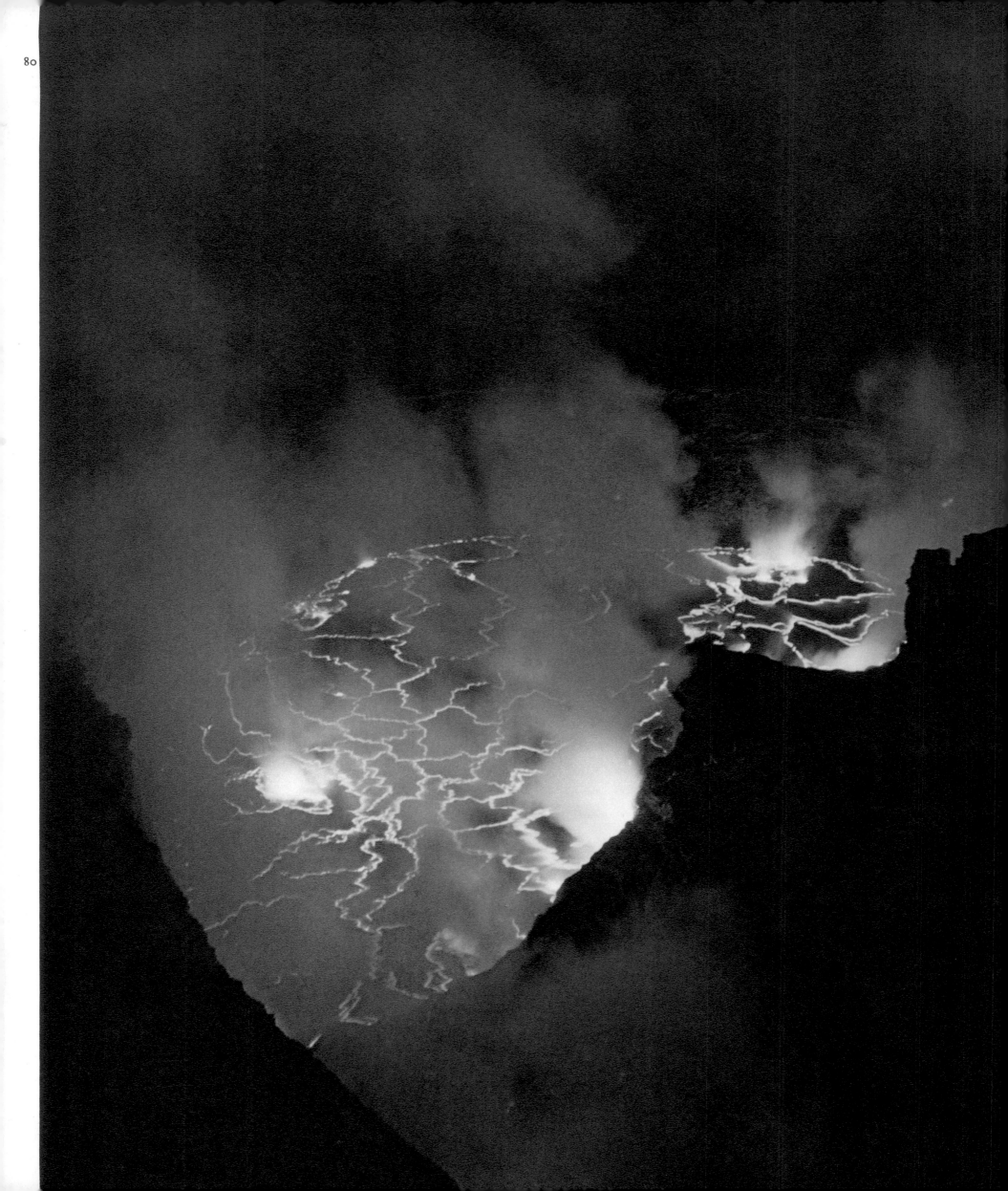

contribute to the eerie unceasing movement of lines and shapes on the boiling lake. Here a broad fountain has just erupted on the western edge of the lake, the thick molten lava has been flung high into the air, and long waves of glowing liquid break against the walls of the crater. More and more vapour rises from the lake until finally the glowing spider's web disappears behind a veil of smoke.

"Pyrometric measurements show that the temperature of the glowing red fissures on the black surface (easily fusible, feldspathic lava with a SiO_2 content of 40 per cent) can reach some 1,470 °F. However, temperatures over 1,700 °F. and a maximum temperature of 1,785 °F. have been recorded in the burning gases of erupting fountains. From the observation platform, which is 650 feet above the lava lake measuring 47,840 square yards, the heat radiation feels like a severe sunburn on one's face. Enough energy is stored here to supply a medium-sized city with electricity. There are 'permanent' and 'secondary' fountains. The former regularly appear in the same spots and mark the vents through which lava rises from the depths. At the peak of outbreak such fountains can spout bits of lava up to 65 feet into the air. The 'secondary' fountains are much smaller and do not last so long. They move with the current of the lake and are caused by the release of gas trapped in bubbles. A mighty mass of rock has been pushed out of the surface of the lower shelf and now floats at an angle in the boiling lava, like an iceberg in water. Impressive changes in Nyiragongo have been recorded by science and research in the course of this century. When Graf von Götzen discovered the crater in 1894, it had two vents. The oldest photograph, taken in 1905 by the Swiss surveyor Thevoz, shows that the two vents had become much wider and that the formation of one large crater had already begun with the collapse of the dividing wall between them. In 1911, the two vents could still be identified, but seven years later they had melted together to form the opening as it is known today. The volcano was dormant for a short time early in 1924, and the present 'lower' platform was created when the lava lake solidified. When the lava lake became active again at the end of 1926, the western section melted away and the eastern section was raised, thus forming the present island of rock. In the last months of 1956, shortly after the photographs shown here had been taken, the lake receded some 115 feet, but later rose again considerably. Here we can see the eternal primary forces of nature at work, and they present us with an impressive picture of the history of the earth."

81 *The hill country of Rwanda.*   An open, pleasant, park-like landscape, with carefully cultivated terraces. This is the home of the tall Watusi people.

82 *Impala, topi, and Grant zebras in Kagera Park, Rwanda.*   "The topi (in the middle of the picture)," writes Heini Hediger, "are the size of a heavy stag and have a curious characteristic peculiar to their species which is difficult to describe: they pose as if for a picture. Although it is biologically utter nonsense, it looks as if they were trying to pose for the camera to their best advantage individually or in small groups and to set themselves up in a picturesque and charming composition with the landscape as a backdrop. Also typical of these animals is the movement of the tail in flight. Contrary to other species of antelopes, topi run with their tails between their legs like dogs and also leap and caper about much more than circumstances would seem to justify. One can confidently speak here of motor extravagances such as are rarely found among wild animals.
"The graceful impala, or black-heeled antelope, also shows exaggerated behaviour in flight, which could be considered a luxury. But while the topi gives vent to its feelings horizontally, the impala expresses itself vertically, in the air. When severely startled, it can clear a car, suddenly leap straight up into the air, or soar thirty-five feet in one graceful bound."
The shy zebras have also retreated to the animal reserves, where well-nourished herds of them are to be found. Although they all seem to look alike with their patterns of stripes, they have individual markings by which they can easily be distinguished upon closer observation. Their conspicuous markings are in great contrast to their natural environment and contradict all theories regarding the natural camouflage of wild animals, even more so since they are a favourite prey of lions because of their distinctive stripes which can so easily be recognized at great distances. On the other hand, it is most difficult to approach a herd of grazing zebras, because they have a very keen sense of sight.

83 *Tall papyrus plants, Uganda.*   For hundreds of miles the young White Nile flows through flat swamplands, which are the most outspoken feature of this region. The most striking and common plant in these swamps is the papyrus, a reed, whose stiff stalks shoot up to a height of five feet, forming a kind of forest. The stems sprout out of turf, three and a half feet thick, which consists of the roots of shrubs and bushes and dead plant matter. The triangular stalks are crowned by a delicate bundle of paper-thin leaves and inflorescences. These plants grow so close together that they form a dense thicket which is impassable unless a path is cut through the stalks—and such a path is, of course, overgrown in no time.
Our paper is named after the papyrus plant. In ancient times the Egyptians cultivated papyrus, and the paper made from this plant was used even as late as the Middle Ages. The pith of the plant was cut into thin strips, which were pasted crosswise on top of each other to form sheets. Scrolls of such sheets were called "papyri" and were the forerunners of the modern book.

84 *Three phases of the sun rising vertically at the equator, Lake George, Uganda.*   At the equinox the sun rises above the horizon at the equator at 6:00 A.M. at 90 degrees east, climbs vertically in a dead-straight line, reaches its zenith at 12 noon, plummets down to the horizon again in a vertical line, and disappears below the horizon at 6:00 P.M. at 270 degrees west. These three phases of the vertically rising sun were taken with a focal length of 1,500 mm at intervals of three minutes.

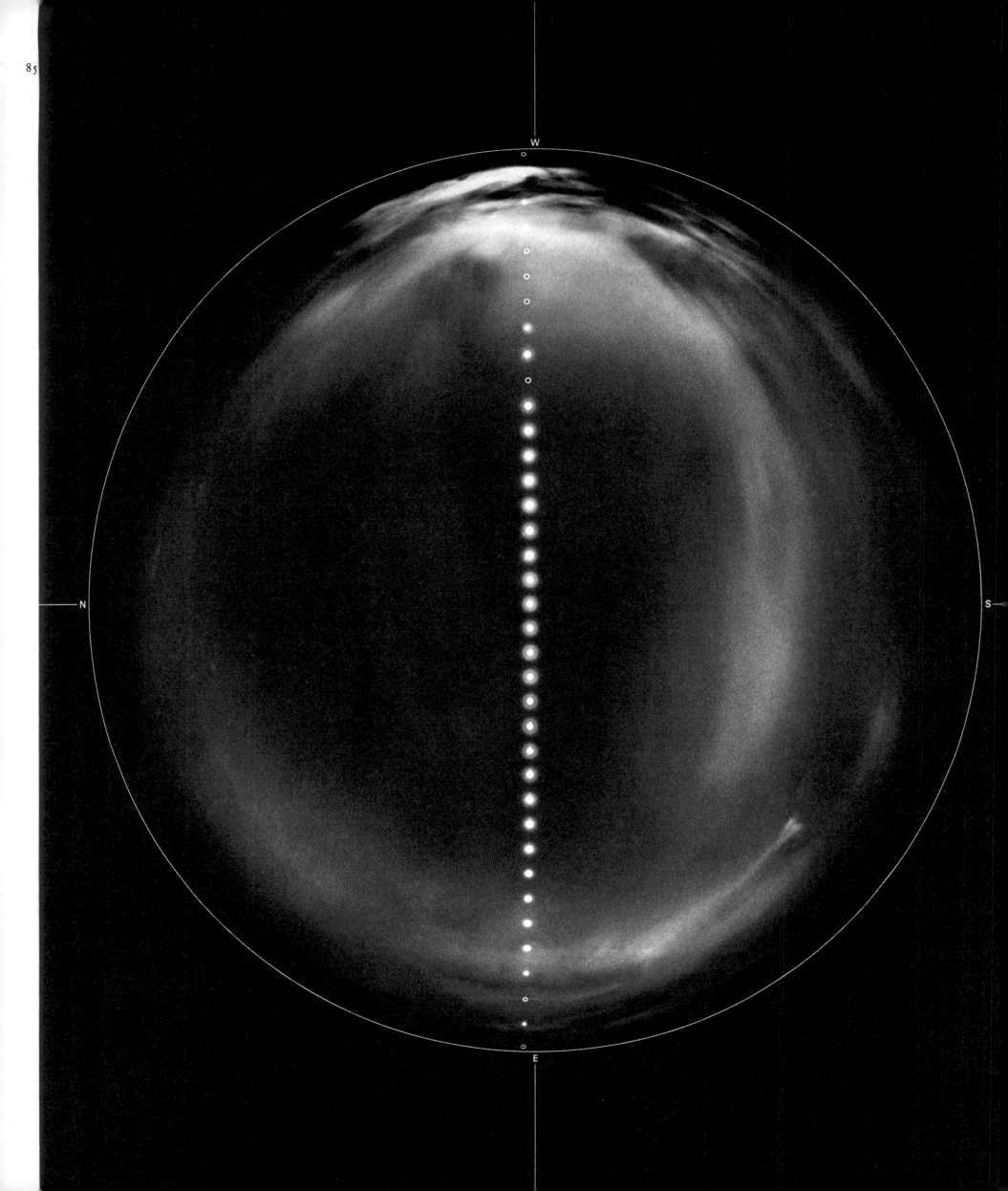

85 *Course of the sun at the equator, Lake George, Uganda.*   This series was taken on March 25 — that is, immediately following the equinox — with a fish-eye camera from 6:00 A.M. to 6:00 P.M. at intervals of 20 minutes. Those positions of the sun which could not be photographed because of cloud formations are indicated on the print with circles. The sun is enlarged because of unavoidable overexposure. The horizontally positioned camera records the celestial hemisphere on a circular disk with the zenith in the middle and the horizon on the periphery. It is, therefore, impossible to avoid distortion. Had the exposures been made on March 20 (the vernal equinox) or September 23 (the autumnal equinox), the series of pictures would have lain exactly on the east-zenith-west line. But after these dates the sun appears in the sky 0° 23' degrees farther north (or south, as the case may be) every day, so that on March 25 the path of the sun lies slightly to the north of the zenith. The sun rises and sets somewhat farther north at the points E and O because of the above-mentioned distortion.

The following is from Emil Schulthess' logbook:

"18th March.   We are at Lake George at the station of an English fishing company, which is situated exactly on the equator at a spot said to have a very steady climate. A location must be found for the cameras where the view is as unobstructed as possible on all sides.

"19th March.   A location has been found one and a half miles from the station. We have set up our equipment on the open plain on the shores of the lake. So that it will not be knocked down by elephants, buffalo, hippopotamuses, or lions roaming about the plains, we have built an enclosure out of iron posts and barbed wire.

"20th March.   I woke up between 2:00 and 3:00 A.M. to the sound of a violent thunderstorm. The alarm went off at 4:45 A.M. It rained in sheets the whole day, while the sun followed its straight path above our heads hidden behind thick layers of clouds.

"21st March.   A glance out of the window; the weather may turn out to be good today. I drive off quickly in the darkness and carefully make all the preparations. But soon the yellowish sky on the horizon reveals a bank of clouds which rises higher and higher; it is cloudy all day long.

"22nd March.   Rain…

"23rd March.   In the early-morning hours the rain pelts down on the roof, just like yesterday. It is so frustrating! The weather clears a bit around 10 o'clock; I drive to our location. Three elephants pass by near the shore. Later on, a buffalo approaches from the east. I manage to photograph it at a distance of only 65 feet. The sun finally comes out shortly before noon, so that I can at least get a picture of it at its zenith with the fish-eye camera.

"24th March.   Rain again. A perfectly hopeless day.

"25th March.   The sky is a delicate red in the east. Following my own tracks, I drive round a tall bush and almost collide with two hippopotamuses, their eyes glowing red in the darkness. I hope that I shall finally be able to get the series with the fish-eye camera. The sun is to rise at exactly 6:00 A.M., but there is a narrow streak of clouds on the horizon again. Then the weather improves noticeably and I am able to make the first exposure at 6:20. But the second one at 6:40 has to be dropped. Then finally, although cloud after cloud drifts across the sky, luck is on my side, and I am able to photograph all the other positions of the sun. It is unbearably hot, and the cameras are so hot that it is almost impossible to handle them. After every exposure, I make a quick retreat to the shade of the car. Shortly before 3:00 P.M. black clouds cover the sun, and suddenly it begins to rain. I refuse to give up, and the sky clears enough to permit me to make the 3:20 and 3:40 P.M. exposures. The following three cannot be made, but then the clouds scatter again. Shortly before 6:00 P.M. the sun sets in the west behind a bank of clouds.

86 *A marabou on the shore of the Victoria Nile, Uganda.* This bird of the stork family is reputed to be exceedingly greedy. Its home is on the plain and along waterways. Near cities and towns the marabou serves as a hygienic garbage collector. Here this bird casually spreads out its mighty wings in the sun; its flesh-coloured head covered with short hairlike feathers and scabby shimmering skin is lowered; its grey-green eyes examine the ground with great concentration in search of anything edible. The marabou nimbly snaps up whatever it finds with its dirty yellowish-white beak, then throws back its head, and the food disappears into its crop.

The Nile, almost 4,160 miles in length, is the longest river in the world. The expression "Father Nile" is in many respects most appropriate. The Victoria Nile is still very "young," but it has already travelled 320 miles trickling down from its source in the mountains of Rwanda and Burundi and traversing Victoria Lake. In the mountains it is called the Kagera Nile; here, the Victoria Nile. But an incredibly magnificent phenomenon lies ahead. At Khartoum the Blue Nile, from Ethiopia, joins this river as it flows along its curiously terraced bed on and on down to Egypt, to which our civilization is so greatly indebted. And without the Nile, ancient Egypt would never have been able to attain such heights. "*Aut Nilus aut nihil*"—either the Nile or nothing. But near Victoria Lake there is certainly no hint of the great wonders and achievements still to come at the other end.

However, there are very early indications of rumours regarding this lake and its location: "In the ninth century, when Emir Ahmed ibn Tulun asked a Coptic hermit about the source of the Nile, he was given the following extraordinary reply: 'The source of the Nile is a large lake not far from that country where day and night are the same all year round.' But in 1857, when Richard F. Burton and John H. Speke set off from Zanzibar to investigate reports of snow-capped mountains and great inland lakes on the equator, the Roman phrase, *caput Nili quaerere*—'to seek the source of the Nile'—had by no means lost the connotation of an exceedingly daring, nay, even impossible feat."—Georg Gerster.

87/88 *Nile crocodile near Murchison Falls, Uganda.* There are twenty different species of crocodile, some of which grow to a length of twenty-five feet. Anyone who takes a closer look at these animals can understand the belief of the Moslems along the Nile that the crocodile is "the son, grandson and great-grandson of that which is damned by Allah." The crocodiles have favourite places where they live, often in surprising proximity with hippopotamuses. They are never far from the water and can often be seen lying on small sandbanks or on islands of grass in the partial shade of trees and bushes, with their gaping jaws and their powerful flat tails draped off the edge of the bank and hanging in the water. They usually lie parallel to the river or face it directly, since water—the element in which the crocodile is really at home—is its means of escape in case of danger.

Of all beasts of prey, crocodiles are considered the greatest threat to human beings. But the seriousness of this threat varies in proportion to the quantity of suitable prey available. Where there are many fish, crocodiles play an important role in maintaining the balance of nature, because they feed on fish, such as catfish, which prey upon many valuable nonpredatory fish. The young also are useful, because they devour the larvae of insects.

The powerful, frightening impression made by "the sons, grandsons, and great-grandsons of that which is damned by Allah" has already been described most dramatically in the Bible. For his servant, Job, the Lord draws a picture of this monster that could hardly be more graphic: "Canst thou draw out leviathan with an hook? or his tongue with a cord which thou lettest down? Canst thou put an hook into his nose? or bore his jaw through with a thorn? Will he

make many supplications unto thee? will he speak soft words unto thee?... Lay thine hand upon him, remember the battle, do no more. Behold, the hope of him is in vain: shall not one be cast down even at the sight of him?... Who can discover the face of his garment? Or who can come to him with his double bridle? Who can open the doors of his face? His teeth are terrible round about. His scales are his pride, shut up together as with a close seal. One is so near to another, that no air can come between them. They are joined one to another, they stick together, that they cannot be sundered. By his sneezings a light doth shine, and his eyes are like the eyelids of the morning. Out of his mouth go burning lamps, and sparks of fire leap out. Out of his nostrils goeth smoke, as out of a seething pot or cauldron. His breath kindleth coals, and a flame goeth out of his mouth. In his neck remaineth strength, and sorrow is turned into joy before him."

89 *Burchell's zebras in Nairobi Park, Kenya.* This species of zebra can be found from northern Kenya all the way down to the Zambezi. The stripe pattern continues from the neck into the mane. All attempts to domesticate the zebra have failed. Even the zebroid, a cross between a zebra and a donkey or a horse, is useful only as an interesting object of study, never as a domestic animal.

Moreover, in certain parts of Africa, the existence of these animals is endangered. For example, countless zebras lost their lives in Miombo through a scientific error. A bitter campain against the plague of tsetse flies was in progress and the zebra was believed to be partially responsible. Much too late it was discovered that these flies are particularly attracted by dark-skinned animals, and experiments with zebralike traps revealed a decided lack of interest on the part of the flies. But by this time "operation butcher" had run its course—another chapter in the woeful history of our "plundered planet" had been written. The campaign against the tsetse fly was at least a more or less plausible reason for the wretched extermination of great herds of zebras, but ruthless extermination of any kind should never again make sense to reasonable human beings.

90 *Mount Kilimanjaro, Kenya, photographed from Amboseli Park.* The summit of this mighty mountain towers majestically above the landscape of Amboseli Park. For the Masai it is their Olympus, the home of the gods. For the modern white man it has become, thanks to Hemingway's short story, the sophisticated mundane symbol of the globetrotter, and yet there is still an aura of myth about this mountain. Kilimanjaro, a volcanic mountain range, has three peaks. The highest is the Kibo Peak (19,340 feet), which has an icecap all year round. It is the so-called parasitic cone between the two older and lower volcanic zones, Mawenzi (17,285 feet) and Schira (14,104 feet).

91 *Amboseli Park, Kenya.* This wide-open dusty landscape is of volcanic origin and lies in the northern shadow of Kilimanjaro. The 1,000 square miles of this park include some of the most beautiful landscapes in Central East Africa. The small black hummocks are the remains of lava which has not yet been completely worn away by erosion. However, the vegetation has long since taken possession of them. Scattered over the open countryside are forests of fever trees (a species of acacia), with their shimmering yellow bark and marshlands with thickets of papyrus and thorn hedges, while in between stretch endless tracts of grassland.

92/93   *Elephant herd in Amboseli Park, Kenya.*   It is not unusual to come across herds of elephants of up to one hundred members. The animals often look as though they were shrouded in a veil in the acacia forest, as they suck up pounds of the fine ashy dust with their trunks and with great gusto blow it out in clouds over their heads and bodies to clean themselves. They roam, grazing, and the countryside looks quite different after they have passed through it. Elephants are gluttons and if their habitat were restricted, it would soon be stripped of all vegetation. For this reason it is virtually impossible to maintain elephants in zoos in an environment resembling their natural habitat. Hence the importance of large reserves. Though even here the influence of these two- and three-ton animals on their environment is most striking. They eat the grass, fell trees, strip the bark off tree-trunks, and remove the foliage from the tops of the lower trees. They maintain meticulous order in their own territories, and if, for example, a tree has fallen across one of their paths, they immediately push it out of the way, thus making "roads" across the territory. In certain areas elephants also bore for water, using their feet to deepen shallow pools as much as possible in order to obtain clear drinking water.

94   *Cow elephant grazing in Amboseli Park, Kenya.*   "The psychomotor intelligence of the elephant, a creature that has no arms to serve it, concentrates on one instrument—its trunk" (Robert Sommer, psychiatrist and animal psychologist).
Photographs like this make Africa look like an animal paradise. Such pictures certainly are beautiful, but we must not let them obscure for us the other side of Africa, the Africa which is being ravaged and plundered systematically. These elephants are living on reserves and the photograph is deceptive. Untiringly the conservationist Heini Hediger admonishes people travelling through Africa today not to succumb to the illusion that the animal parks where so much wildlife can be seen—"these vital reservoirs which are damming the flow of destruction" —prove the situation to be less grave than it is claimed to be. "The world beyond these sanctuaries often has precious little left in common with paradise; many regions are desolate, emptied by the hunter of all signs of life. In the last century alone most of the larger wild animals which once inhabited Africa have been destroyed, and the survivors have had to forfeit the greater part of the territory that was once their domain. Innumerable species are lost forever; many others are in danger of becoming extinct. African wildlife is actually on the decrease. All factors contributing to this state of affairs, that constitute an additional threat to the reserves, should be meticulously examined; this includes every shot that is fired, every tree that is felled, every new road. It is high time that an acceptable compromise be found, in which neither the existence of man or animal is fatally threatened."

95   *Black rhinoceros with young in Amboseli Park, Kenya.*   This young rhinoceros, about a year and a half old, has no horns yet, but there is already a lump on its nose where the frontal horn will appear. Young rhinoceros are very active. It is interesting to observe how the mother animal "speaks" to her young, guiding it with blowing and snorting sounds, hurrying it when it lags behind, and fetching it back when it has run on ahead. The importance of aural communication is demonstrated by the fact that the young rhinoceros always has its ears turned in the direction of the mother animal. There is a curious symbiosis between these animals and the oxpecker. Rhinoceros are always accompanied by these birds which feed on the annoying parasites that infest their hide, but also peck mercilessly at wounds caused by the parasites, thus tormenting the animal. Oxpeckers are not easily frightened and the rhinoceros is in fact defenceless against them.

96 *Black rhinoceros bull in Amboseli Park, Kenya.* The Black rhinoceros bull is exceedingly dangerous. If it is startled in the underbush, it attacks immediately. The Black rhinoceros is no darker than the White rhinoceros; both species are grey, but whereas the Black rhinoceros has pointed lips, the White rhinoceros is square-lipped. These animals are also threatened with extinction all over the world. Their meat, teeth and skin are not in demand, fashion has left these by the wayside; it is their horn that is so coveted. In the Orient even their tracks are believed to be endowed with the power to heal and as a result the Indian rhinoceros has been completely wiped out. But merchants have no qualms about importing rhinoceros from Africa and are quite literally prepared to pay for their weight in gold.

97 *A mound built by termites in Tsavo Park, Kenya.* Ever since termites were introduced into the white man's world, they have had a thoroughly bad reputation. They are notorious for destroying wood, and whole cities have been threatened with destruction by these insects. In Africa termites usually live in their own houses, seldom invading those of others. They live in extraordinarily complex colonies of often more than a million insects. Their mounds are frequently several yards high and have a highly sophisticated internal architecture with water canals, air shafts, and tunnels for transport. As building materials, termites use a mixture of earth and saliva which is as hard as cement when it dries; and they also use their own excrement consisting of digested wood particles. Termites are a favourite prey of birds, but other animals, such as chimpanzees, also like them. The aardvark feeds almost exclusively on termites; its very strong claws are capable of digging into the hardest of termite citadels. Zebras are also fond of these mounds against which they scratch their hide, and even elephants rub themselves against them in places where there are no trees at their disposal.

98/99   *Masai herdsman and Masai herds in Amboseli Park, Kenya.*   Today the proud Masai live on a reservation. "The Masai are nomads of Hamitic origin, who wander across vast regions of the half waterless flats of Kenya and Tanzania," writes L.S.B. Leakey, the outstanding expert on the tribes in this region. "A small part of their territory has a relatively good water supply, for example, the Ngorongoro highlands of Tanzania or the mountain forests of Mau in Kenya. Extensive areas, however, are extremely dry except for the rainy season in March, April and May, and for a further month or two. During the rainy season the Masai families move with their cattle across the plains, trying to take as much advantage as possible of the temporarily succulent grass and the plentiful water. But as the dry season progresses, they are forced to gather together at the few spots where enough water is available for their large herds.

"These large herds are a necessity for them; not simply a symbol of wealth, as many believe, but rather their principal source—in the most literal sense of the word—of nourishment. Blood constitutes a substantial part of their diet—and not blood taken from the slaughtered animal, but from the veins of the living creature. If the pastureland is good during the rainy season, blood can be taken from an animal once every ten days; but during the dry season the animals can only be bled every forty days without becoming emaciated. In other words, no less than forty head of cattle per person are required to supply each member of the family with the principal meal of the day. Simple arithmetic thus shows that 200 head of cattle are required for a family of five—but an average Masai family with grandparents, aunts and cousins usually comes to about twenty, and that means about 800 head of cattle.

"Tourists frequently ask why there are so many oxen, and even old oxen, among the herds of the Masai. Why don't the Masai slaughter these useless animals, which simply devour grass and claim their share of the limited water supply? For the white farmer, oxen and barren cows are merely creatures to be fattened up and later slaughtered for their meat. But for the Masai every animal is a principal source of nourishment as long as it is alive and healthy.

"To bleed the live animal, it is first tied up and then a leather strap is wound around its neck like a tourniquet, so that a large ball of blood swells up on the side of the neck. This swollen blood-vessel is then pierced with a special arrow and the blood that spurts out is collected in a bottle-gourd. A little juice from a wild plant is added to make the blood coagulate and when it has thickened, it is cooked like liver. For most Masai this coagulated blood is the principal ingredient of their diet. It is washed down with fresh milk, flavoured with a dash of cow urine."

100/101   *Young Masai woman and Masai youth, Amboseli Park, Kenya.*   This girl's short curly hair is thickly plastered with ochre dust. The hair-style of the youth is typical of the Masai—countless tiny braids wound together in bundles. Both wear the characteristic earrings. Should the two wish to greet each other, the girl would lower her head slightly and the young man gently touch her forehead with two fingertips. Before marriage, the young Masai warriors live in complete sexual freedom with the young women of their community. Even married women are encouraged to have several lovers. The Masai marriage has nothing to do with sex-life; it simply determines who is responsible for home, family, and food supply. Therefore, it often happens that a Masai father may be the real father of perhaps only one of his wife's many children, but this in no way interferes with the peace of the family.

Tribes living very close to the Masai have gone through an astonishing development in only a few decades and this has made the new Africa possible; but the Masai themselves are extremely backward. They stubbornly persist in living in the Iron Age. L.S.B. Leakey has investigated this backwardness: "Is it because they are incapable of participating in the progress

of civilization? Or is it because as a community they feel a collective aversion to what we call civilization? The answer is not that they are inherently incapable of making progress, but that the values of European civilization regarding progress mean nothing to them. Whether this is right or wrong is quite another question. From time to time a few, a very few Masai have chosen the path of civilization, which has already been travelled by the members of so many other tribes in East Africa, such as the Kikuyu, the Baganda and the Chagga. However, those few Masai have demonstrated beyond a doubt that they are perfectly capable of taking advantage of their education and that it is only a matter of will.

"I know a Masai who is an excellent mechanic for internal combustion engines and who speaks English, French, German, Hindustani and Swahili in addition to his own dialect. He also plays a good game of chess. I know another Masai who was educated in London and is now a brilliant surgeon, who is also successful in many other fields of medicine. Such men are rare among the Masai, but they prove how much potential there is in this tribe. The difficulty lies in the fact that the Masai people as a whole are not the least bit interested in making this kind of progress. Today an increasing number of Masai children are attending school. They learn the same things that children from other tribes learn. For a certain length of time they wear the school uniform and with proper guidance they lead a tidy, hygienic, orderly life, but as soon as their schooldays are over, everything they have learned is like water rolling off a duck's back, and the majority of them return to their tribal life as if nothing whatsoever had intervened."

102   *A herd of giraffes in flight near Loitokitok, Kenya.*

103   *The Mzima Springs in Tsavo National Park, Kenya.*   Crystal-clear water bubbles out of crevices in rocks of solidified lava.

104   *Hippopotamus, Mzima Springs, Tsavo National Park, Kenya.*   This is the only place in the world where hippopotamuses are known to live in clear water. During the day these amphibious vegetarians normally prefer muddy waters and the banks of rivers.

105 *Tracks made by a turtle in the sand on the Indian Ocean, Tanzania.* This huge animal has come ashore to lay its eggs in the sand. The tracks it has made across the sand resemble those of a caterpillar tractor. With unerring instinct, this animal lays its eggs beyond reach of high tide and breakers; it lays over a hundred eggs which are about the size of ping-pong balls and have leathery shells. They are a great find for the natives who fry the yolks.

106 *A hammerhead shark from the Indian Ocean, Tanzania.* These fishermen from Kigombe—a charming village a few miles south of Tanga—have made a very good catch.

107 *Dew on the bush in the tropical zone.* In the lowlands and mountains of the "hot-house" tropics, dew falls at night on the bush and in the jungle, moistening every leaf, blossom, straw and twig. But only the early riser experiences the enchantment of this glistening splendour; the rising sun soon absorbs every drop of moisture.

108 *Primeval forest in the Usambara Mountains, Mazumbai, Tanzania.* The most beautiful part of this virgin mountain forest has recently been declared the Mazumbai Natural Forest Reserve and now belongs to the University of Dar es Salaam. In this way it has not only been rescued from the insatiable and ever-increasing demands of man, but it has also been dedicated to scientific research and investigation.

The Usambara forest is famous for its luxuriant vegetation. The beautiful blossoms of the parasitic plants and the patterns made by the delicate green ferns gleam and shimmer in the gloom of the forest. Colours, shapes, sizes—everything seems to be in excess. The domelike tops of the gigantic trees have a span of some 150 to 200 feet. And an audible silence, peculiar to the jungle, stirs below. The human ear seems to hear the very voice of the forest itself: tree trunks swaying in the wind rub against each other, playing the bass with the primeval melody of the jungle rising above.

109 *Baobabs (monkey-bread trees) near M'Bugwe, Tanzania.* Naked as always during the dry season, the branches of this silk-cotton tree are silhouetted against the sky. This tree, incidentally, has many uses: the pulp of the gourdlike fruit is edible, the leaves yield a vegetable similar to spinach, the oil from the seeds is used to make lard, the bark to make ropes and cloth, while the fibre of the fruit yields silk-cotton, and the wood is used for canoes. Baobabs are probably among the oldest living plants in the world; specimens have been found which are estimated to be two thousand years old. Another curiosity is that the trunks of giant specimens some sixty-five feet high can be just as broad as the trees are tall. Furthermore, these huge trunks consist of spongy wood tissue estimated to contain 26,400 gallons of water, and are so soft that a bullet can easily pass straight through them. The tree is protected from loss of water by a thick shiny grey bark, and by its small leaves and dead foliage.

110 *Landscape near Kondoa Iringa, Tanzania.* "This strangely melancholy landscape, characterized by mighty baobabs and Candelabra Euphorbia, is actually a sad ruin of a landscape which at the time of Germany's annexation of East Africa was one of the most fertile districts in the whole colony," writes Peter R.O. Bally. He attributes this metamorphosis to the "uncontrolled excessive demands made on the land by man and animal." Since it was virtually robbed of all vegetation, the land became exposed to erosion caused by wind and rain.

Just as the zoologists lament the sometimes ruthless extermination of Africa's wildlife, so the botanists lament the loss of vegetation. Bally insists that no effort is too great to bring about a

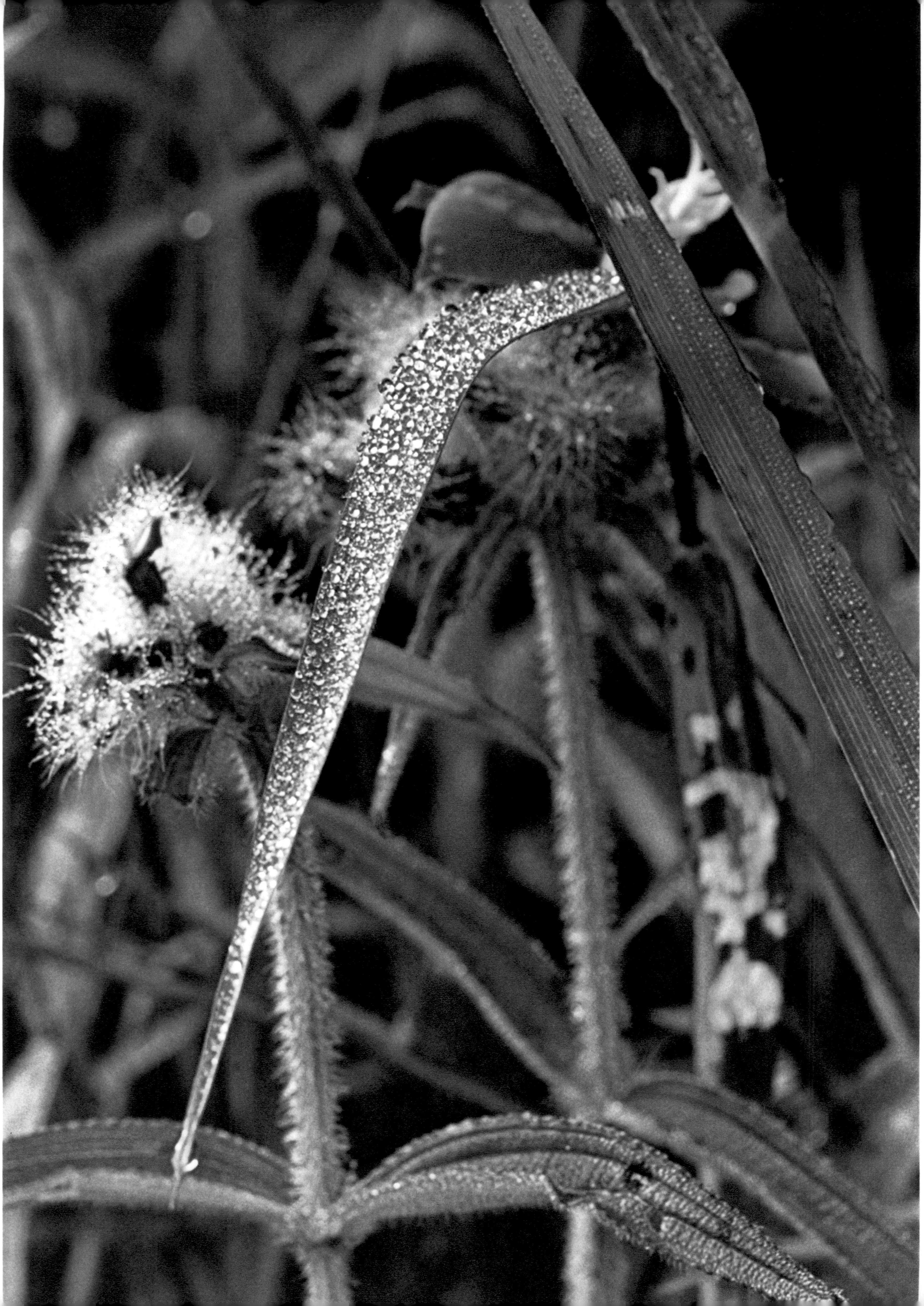

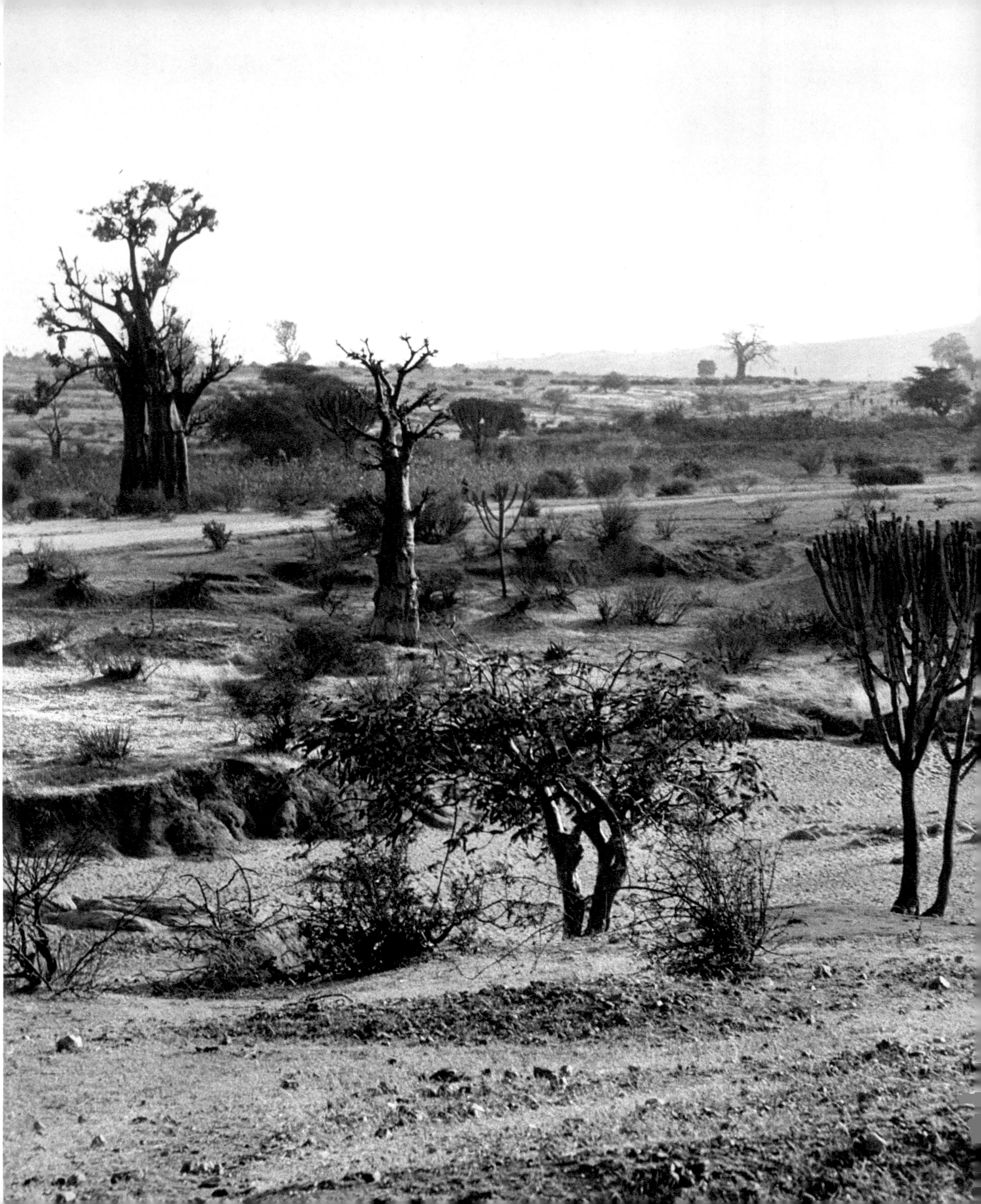

worldwide awareness of the immeasurable value of the conservation of nature: "The distribution of the vegetation across the African continent is familiar to everyone in its broad outlines—the vast deserts in the north and southwest, whose sandy barren wastes form such a contrast to the luxuriant, hot and humid tropical belt of the west and the savannahs of the east, which are so rich in game. And probably everyone has heard of the fertile highlands in East Africa, Rhodesia, and the Republic of South Africa, which, with their moderate climate, can be compared to Europe in many respects. It is fallacious, however, to assume that this distribution is determined by nature, that it is only caused by changes on the earth's surface over thousands of centuries, dating back to geological epochs, or even that it has remained unchanged since history has been recorded. In history lessons in school we learned that large parts of North Africa such as the Carthage of long ago, Libya and neighbouring countries have for the most part turned into desert, but were once the granaries of ancient Rome; and even today the ruins of cities are an imposing reminder of the fertility of these tracts of land, which once not only maintained a large population, but were also so productive that export was possible. The untold thousands of wild animals which appeared in Roman circuses—elephants, lions, giraffes, and others—came for the most part from North Africa, where the vegetation today is far too scanty to support such a wealth of wildlife. We learned at the same time that the land was ravaged, the waterways dried up, and the mountains stripped of vegetation due to ignorance and lack of foresight on the part of the ancient inhabitants of those regions. We also took it for granted that our modern knowledge in the areas of agriculture, forestry and the conservation of the earth's fertility would never allow such devastating consequences.

"Nothing could be more wrong. The destruction of the flora on our planet has probably never progressed more rapidly than at present; the devastation in Africa from south of the Sahara desert all the way down to the Cape of Good Hope during the last sixty to one hundred years is without a doubt greater than during the past two thousand years—and this in spite of the fact that experts have long known perfectly well what irrevocable damage man himself will have to suffer because of this destruction.

"This applies especially to East Africa, which was virtually unexplored until the turn of the century. Forests are disappearing everywhere; the bushland is turning into grassland, and pastureland is turning into desert under the pressure of man's 'snowballing' demands on nature. Devastation is spreading so rapidly that the immediate future of entire countries is already most seriously threatened."

Southern Africa

The rise between the Congo basin and the Kalahari depression can easily be distinguished on a relief map of Africa. This second seam, which cuts across the African continent, is not quite as clear-cut as that of the southern edge of the Sahara, but the Katanga rise, as it is called, is by no means insignificant. Here the waters separate into the Congo River system and the Zambezi and Okawango systems. South of the area that we call tropical Africa, year round rains give way to seasonal precipitation. The luxuriant tropical rain forests of the Congo encroach further south only along the rivers; elsewhere the foliage becomes thinner and the forests lighter. Finally the trees give way to flat grasslands and on the horizon the dry Kalahari Desert appears. The sub-tropical world follows, completing the symmetrical arrangement of climatic zones on the African continent.

111   *Sunset on the Great North Road, Zambia.*   Lusaka, the capital of the former British Protectorate of Northern Rhodesia, is surrounded by extremely fertile land, where rice, sunflowers and tobacco are cultivated.

112   *Kudu antelope.*   The animals in this and the following four photographs are to be found in the Wankie Game Reserve, Rhodesia, and in Kruger Park, Republic of South Africa. Both parks have very similar biotopes. Among the innumerable, in fact uncounted, species of antelope, the kudu buck with its lyre-shaped, curving horns makes a very imposing picture. Of particular interest is the pattern of stripes on the hide, which looks as if it had been placed there almost by accident and which often makes it very difficult to distinguish the animal from the surrounding landscape. The kudu was threatened with extinction during the cattle-plague epidemic of 1896, but is now widespread in both the Wankie Game Reserve and Kruger Park. It is often larger than the stag of Central Europe.

113   *Family of giraffes.*

114   *Long-tailed shrike.*   This bird is particularly striking, because, of its total length of twenty inches, the tail alone measures fourteen.

115   *Yellow-billed hornbill.*   A typical inhabitant of thornbush areas.

116   *Cormorant.*   This species ranges over almost all of Africa.

Kruger Park, the largest national park in the world, was established by the president of the former Transvaal Boer Republic. Already in 1884 "Oom Paul," as the Boers affectionately nicknamed Kruger, had drawn up plans to establish a game reserve in the northeastern corner

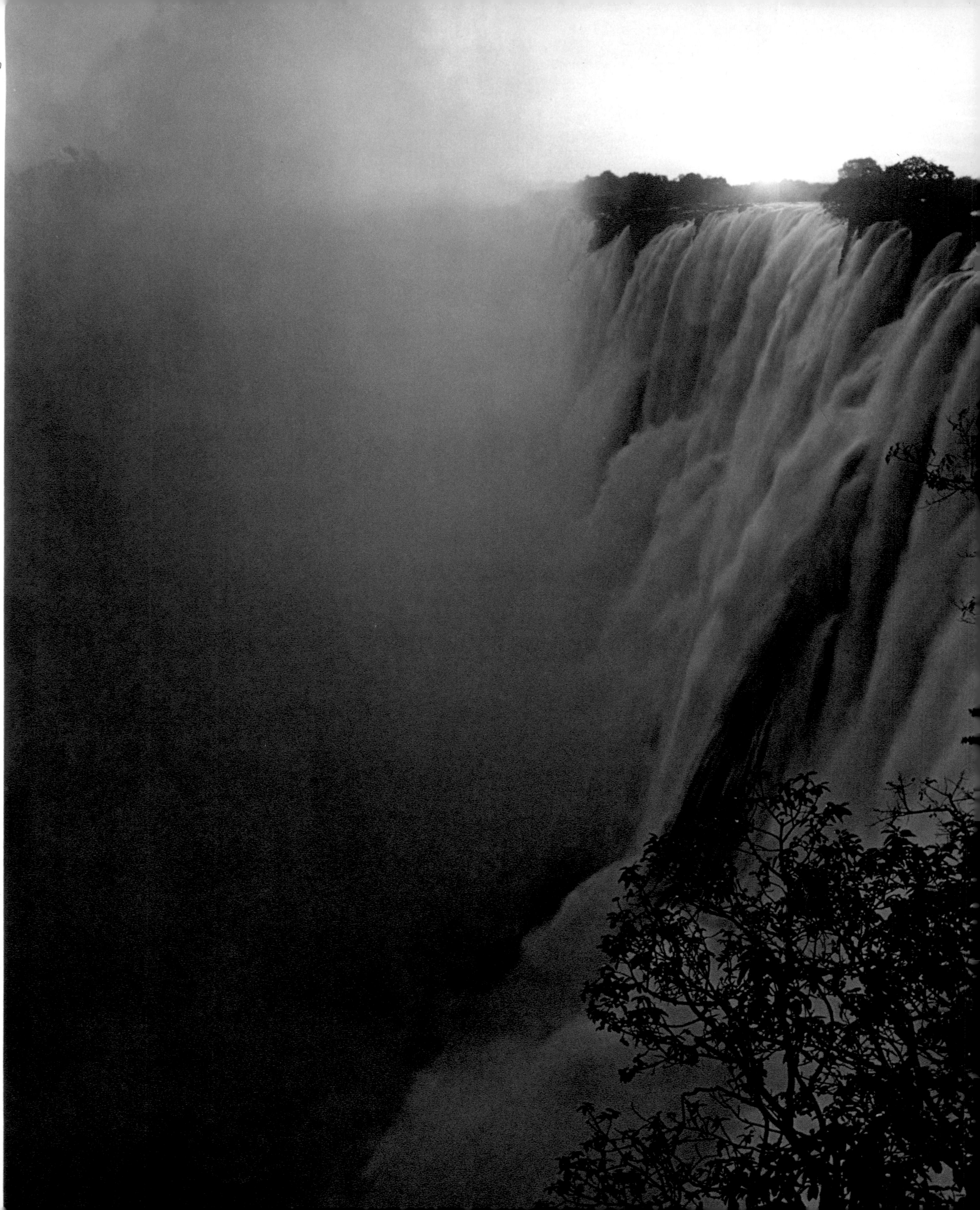

of the Transvaal. This vast project was then converted into reality step by step, until in 1926 it was given its final present-day legal status by vote of the parliament of the former Union of South Africa. Kruger Park covers an area of some 5,950,000 acres, and over a million animals live in the bushland which is 225 miles long and about 40 miles wide. Here there are lions, leopards, cheetahs, jackals, hyenas, wild dogs, elephants, giraffes, zebras, antelopes, buffalo, warthogs, rhinoceros, hippopotamuses, crocodiles, and baboons—just to mention a few! But Kruger Park was not only designed as a wildlife refuge; it is also intended to give man an idea of paradisaic conditions.

117 *Victoria Falls: Main Fall seen from Cataract Island, Zambia.*

118 *Victoria Falls: Main Fall seen from the Rhodesian side.*

119 *The eastern cataract of Victoria Falls at sunset, Zambia.*

The Zambezi, the longest river in southern Africa and nearly 2000 yards wide, flows sluggishly across the African landscape. The first white man to see this river was the eccentric explorer David Livingstone. Brought up in the Scottish village of Blantyre, he started life as a factory worker and later became a medical missionary. Following the course of the river as he did, you will see mighty columns of vapour rising from the river in the distance. These columns announce the Victoria Falls. Suddenly the river plunges foaming and steaming into a gorge 330 feet deep, roaring like ten thousand giants, so that spray climbs up into the sky again like magic and falls on the surrounding greenhouse landscape—an eternal delicate shower of rain.

After its fall, the raging river tumbles through a narrow, zigzag gorge, which then opens up into a broad valley where peace is once again restored. Livingstone believed that the gorge into which the river crashes might be a crevasse caused by a prehistoric earthquake. More recent studies show that the Zambezi itself gouged the falls out of the basalt.

Livingstone's description of the discovery of Victoria Falls in his diary is a gripping example of man's tireless quest for knowledge, of the joy of discovery and of scrupulously meticulous scholarship: "21st November, 1855. Entering canoes on the 13th, some sailed down the river to the confluence of the Chobe, while others drove the cattle along the banks, spending one night at Mparia, the island at the confluence of the Chobe ... Attempting to proceed down the river next day, we were detained some hours by a strong east wind, raising waves so large as to threaten to swamp the canoes ... After one more day we arrived at the falls of Victoria, called by the natives Mosioatunya, or more anciently Shongwe. After 20 minutes' sail from Kalai, we came in sight, for the first time, of the columns of vapour, appropriately called 'smoke,' rising at a distance of five or six miles, exactly as when large tracts of grass are burned in Africa. Five columns now arose, and bending in the direction of the wind, they seemed placed against a low ridge covered with trees ... About half a mile from the falls, I left the canoe by which we had come down thus far, and embarked in a lighter one, with men well-acquainted with the rapids, who, by passing down the centre of the stream in the eddies and the still places caused by many jutting rocks, brought me to an island situated in the middle of the river, and on the edge of the lip over which the water rolls. The entire falls are simply a crack made in a hard basalt rock from the right to the left bank of the Zambezi. In other falls there is usually a great difference in height in the river-bed and the adjacent land bordering it, and the river is more or less the same before and after the falls. Here, however, the river races past innumerable islands and then with its width of 800 to 1000 yards leaps bodily into a gulf a hundred feet deep, where it becomes suddenly compressed into a space of fifteen to twenty yards; is forced there to change its direction, and flow from the right to the left bank; and then rush boiling and roaring through the hills … In some places the lips of the fissure are not more than 50 or 60 feet apart … When the water is low, as now, the falls break up into jets of vapour, mounting 200 or 300 feet high, and breaking up into spray. Of the five columns, two on the right, and one on the left of the island were the largest, and the streams which formed them seemed each to exceed in size the falls of the Clyde at Stonebyres, when the river is in flood. A piece of rock has fallen off a spot on the left of the island, and juts out from the water below, and from it, I judged the distance which the water falls to be about 100 feet. As far as I could guess, there was a flow of five or six hundred yards of water, which, at the edge of the fall, seemed at least three feet deep. My companions entertained themselves by throwing stones into the abyss, and were then astonished when a stone one to two inches in diameter disappeared from sight before it reached the foaming water. I believe that no one could perceive where the vast body of water went; it seemed to lose itself in the earth. The bottom of the eastern half of the fissure, which contains the most water, is never visible. When we peered down over the verge, we could see nothing but a dense white cloud with two bright rainbows in it. When the wind blew eastwards, the constant shower which falls from the columns of vapour soon wetted us to the skin. When the river is full, or in flood, the columns, it is said, can be seen ten miles off and the falls make a very great noise. Then the water is said to shoot up in great waves, which reach all the way to the other edge."

120 *The valley of the Zambezi River, sixty miles below Victoria Falls, Zambia.* This picture of the sluggishly flowing river has disappeared; the magnificent landscape has had to be sacrificed for the reservoir of the Kariba power station. A dam 400 feet high has been constructed in the Kariba gorge, so that now a part of the Zambezi boasts the largest artificial lake in the world: 175 miles long and 42 miles wide. The power station was inaugurated in 1960 and produces eight milliards kw a year. But these impressive figures cannot obscure the fact that 30,000 people living in the area flooded by the dam had to be relocated, not to mention the wild animals which were driven away.

121–123 *Tonga women near Sinazongwe, Zambia.* The old woman is smoking a hookah; the girl is grinding millet on a granite grindstone just the way it was done in the Stone Age; and this young beauty with her ornaments is a perfect illustration of the untouched world of the Tonga tribes. These people had to be resettled to make way for the Kariba dam, and there was even talk of making fishermen of them. In this case "progress" has demanded a very high tribute. The Tonga people, admittedly, did not have a very highly developed culture, but until recently they had succeeded in preserving their primitive way of life with great tenacity. They once belonged to the kingdom of "Mono-Motapa," which still survives in legends and which was governed by a divine king. The following is taken from Bernatzik's *Handbook of African Ethnology*: "This sacred king, whose reign was of limited duration determined by the aristocratic priesthood, had virtually absolute power. He was believed to be the incarnation of a mythical ancestor and, as such, to have power over rain; he was worshipped like a god. His intimate relationship with the moon was established by a series of unmistakable signs. His life and reign were terminated by sacred regicide. Upon his death all the fires in the land were extinguished, to be re-lit under the new king, from whom the vassals formally received it again, thus renewing their subjection to the royal might. The name 'Mono-Motapa' (Mono-

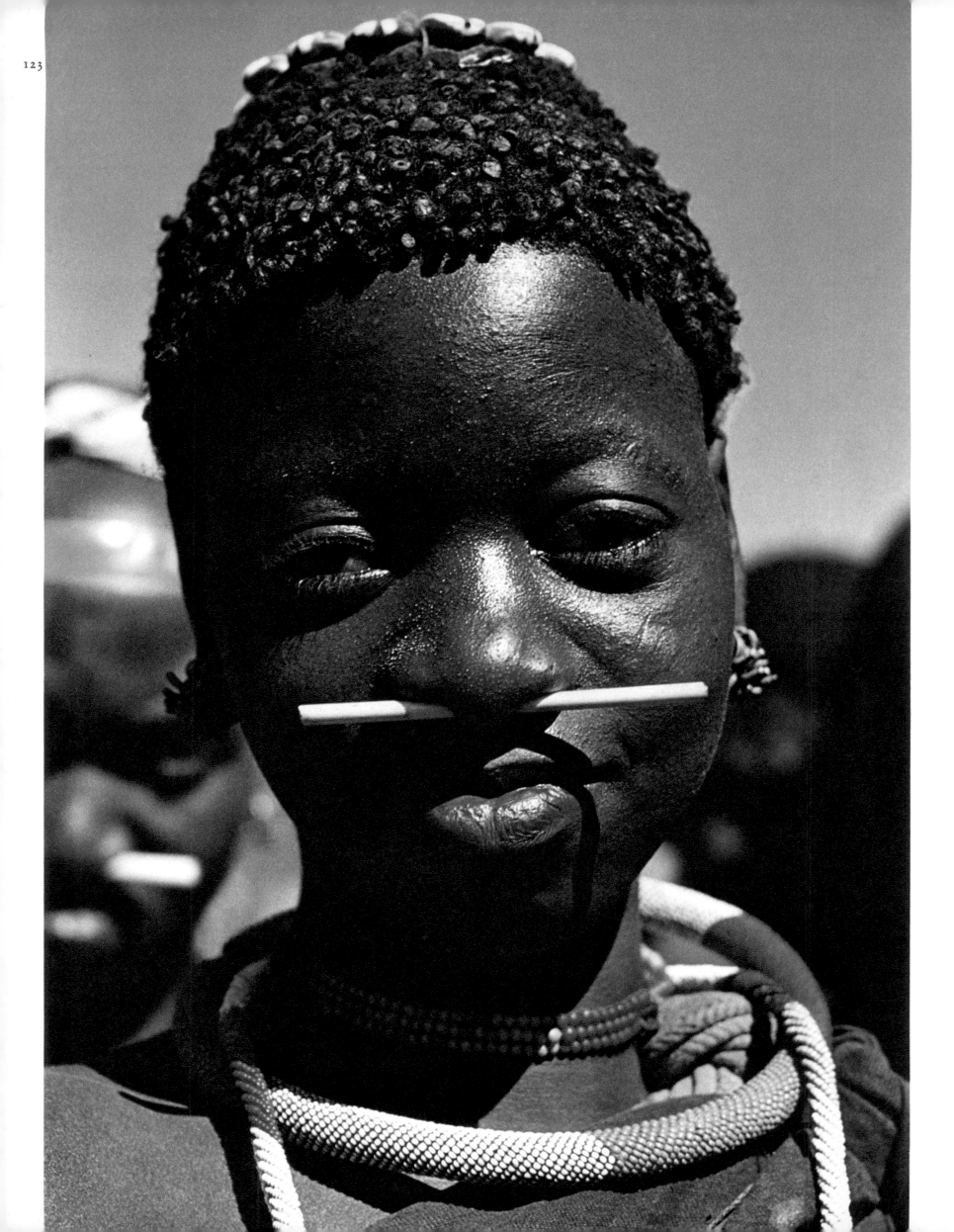

prince) has come down to us from Portuguese accounts. This ruler's kingdom extended over all of Rhodesia and a large part of Mozambique. Numerous civil and foreign wars caused the downfall of this empire …"

124   *Funeral in Siasimuna, Zambia.*   The Tonga funeral rites usually last several days. On a square between the huts men, women and children stamp round in a circle, droning the same monotonous singsong over and over again to the sounds of a drum and a trumpet made out of an antelope horn. Women mourners wail loudly while a few men armed with lances and oval tin shields wildly invoke the spirits. Inevitably, customs like these funeral rites will sooner or later die out, now that the Tonga people have been uprooted from their ancestral homeland.

125   *Rock paintings in Nswatugi Cave in the Matopo Hills near Bulawayo, Rhodesia.*

126   *Rock paintings, Epworth near Salisbury, Rhodesia.*

Paintings found on huge boulders and in rock shelters go under the general designation of Bushman Art. There are differing theories about the age of these paintings. Some scientists date them in the Stone Age and believe them to be related to cave paintings found in southern France and Spain. Other experts judge them to be much more recent, since representations of white men wearing hats are found among them. They are probably paintings of varying age, some being imitations of original Stone Age work by modern Bushmen.
Three styles have been determined in the find near Bulawayo. The first is related to the paintings found in caves in the eastern part of Spain, in which red, yellow and a yellowish-brown are the dominant colours; the second is characterized by the use of only one colour, claret-red, and by the realistic representation of animals; the third style makes use of various colours, including white.
The rock paintings of southern Africa show a marked difference from those of the north. Even the technique is completely different: pictures are scratched into rocks in the north and painted on to them in the south. The manner of representation also differs considerably: monumental in the north; more delicate, graceful, elegant in the south. Human beings often figure in the paintings in the south, but they are not as realistically drawn as the various animals. The tools and techniques of Bushmen painters are described by the archaeologist, A.L. Armstrong, who excavated the Bambata Cave in Rhodesia. "In the middle and upper layers many raw materials for paints were found, consisting of balls and fragments of yellow ochre, as well as drawing implements, fragments and balls of red and brown hematite and ochre. The implements were pear-shaped or triangular and always had distinct scratch-marks on the pointed ends and often on the surfaces and edges as well. These markings were apparently produced by rubbing the implements against a rough surface. Some of the ochre fragments have similar markings; but the balls of yellow ochre and most of the pieces of red ochre are softer and therefore the scrapes have not been preserved, although their shape is obviously artificial and some of them have flat surfaces, which seem to be the result of use … Upon examining the technique of the wall paintings, it was found that animals and figures were usually first drawn in outline, with rather bold contours, which were then filled in by rubbing the rock with the chosen colour, much as a child would use crayons …, therefore these pictures are basically pastels and not paintings. The traces of usage observed correspond exactly to those which would be caused by such a technique, so that there is no doubt that we are here in possession of the remains of some of the tools with which the representations were made."

127–129 *Ndebele Africans, Mapoch, Republic of South Africa.* The village of Mapoch is close to Pretoria, the capital of the Republic. The primitive atmosphere is, however, deceptive, since the village has been placed under the special protection of the state and is in fact a living ethnographical open-air museum, preserved for the benefit of tourists. Nevertheless, the highly developed decorative art of the inhabitants has apparently escaped being much influenced by the outside world, though it is interesting to note that the wall decorations of the Ndebele people still living in the north are far more sober than those of the south. The presence of the Ndebele tribe in the south is due to a charming and moving story. These people lived originally in the northern Transvaal. One day their prince, Mapoch, was summoned to appear in court in Pretoria for some misdemeanour. However, the families under Mapoch's rule could not live without their prince, and so they followed him, setting up camp to the north of Pretoria, to await the release of their lord and master. But as it turned out, they never went back to their tribal hunting grounds. Once a farming people, they now live almost exclusively from the tourist trade. The striking geometrical designs with which their houses are decorated are painted exclusively by women. They once used various ochre colours from the earth, but nowadays they buy their paints in the shops of Pretoria.

130 *"The Land of a Thousand Hills" near Drummond in Natal, Republic of South Africa.* Like waves on the ocean these hills stretch across the landscape behind Durban in the direction of the Indian Ocean. The region of Natal Province was discovered by Vasco da Gama on Christmas Day in 1497, which explains the name of this province since *natal* means Christmas in Portuguese.

131 *Zulus near Durban, Republic of South Africa.* The guitar bears the name "Chaka," in memory of the "black Napoleon," a warring Zulu king who conquered a great territory during the first half of the nineteenth century. These one-time warriors have now become farmers, absorbed by city life and civilization.

132 *Miner in Johannesburg, Republic of South Africa.* In the Republic of South Africa alone, 330,000 Africans are employed in mines. The gold extracted here accounts for almost half of the gold mined in the whole world. In addition there are important diamond mines. A treasury of mineral resources of explosive potential, but the new Africa, in which two worlds must learn to live together, needs time to grow. Peter Sulzer, the Swiss expert on Africa, pleads for understanding: "A great deal of loving understanding is necessary to comprehend the inner riches of the black human being and to help him escape his psychic prison of frustration. A great deal of loving understanding is also required of us to comprehend white South Africa, with whose spiritual interests the world has hardly concerned itself as yet. The world is familiar with South African gold, but not with the South African soul.
"In the belief that peaceful coexistence in the spirit of brotherly love is possible, and out of sympathy with both white and black Africa, I hazard two wishes here: the wish that the white man realize how vital it is to help the black man escape his frustration; and the wish that the European understand how important it is that South Africa also be a permanent home for the white man."

133 *Grazing lands in the Transkei, Republic of South Africa.* Some one and a half million blacks and one hundred thousand whites live in the territory of the Transkei. This is a model illustration of the South African Bantustan policy, that is, the attempt to reserve certain areas of South

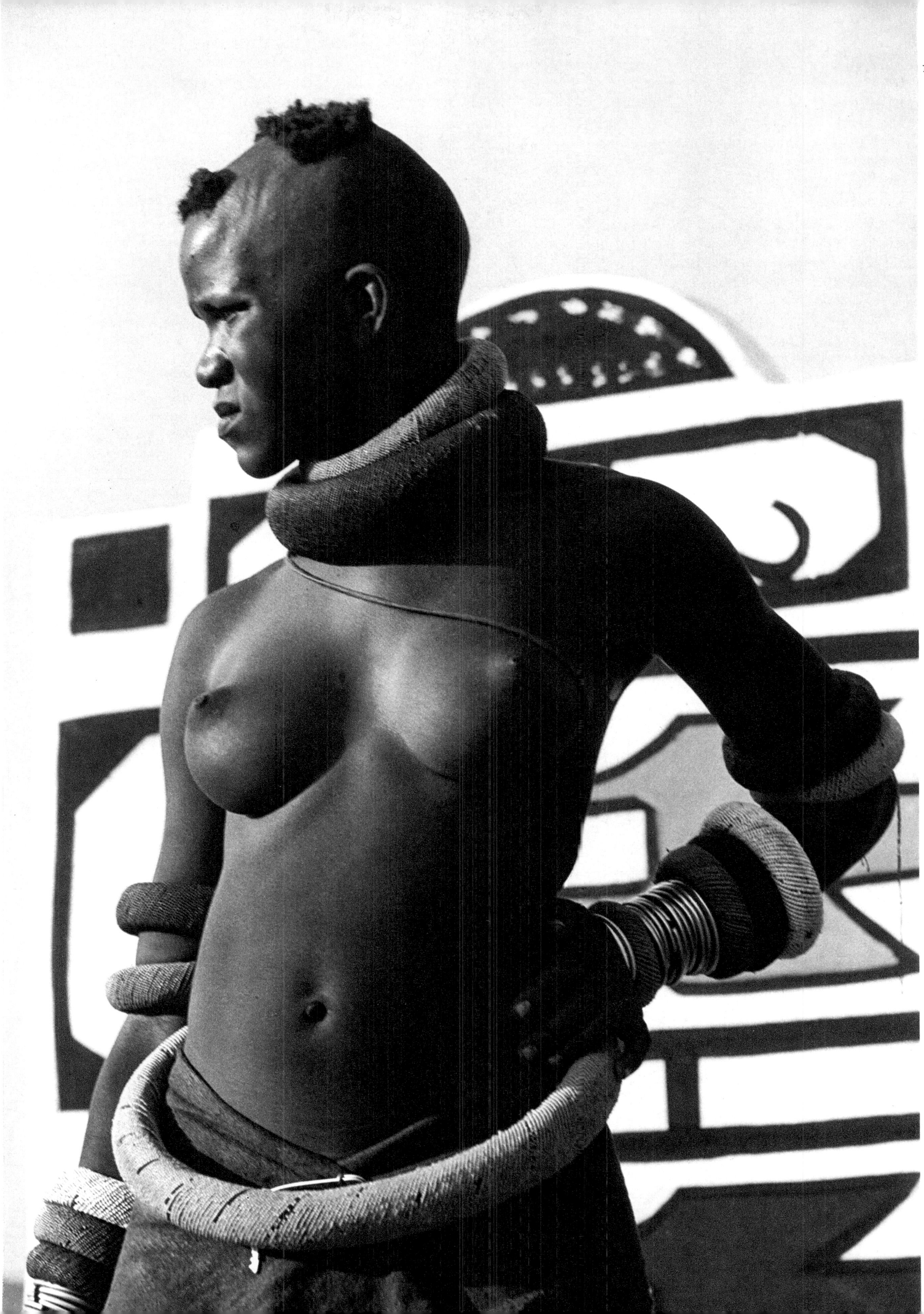

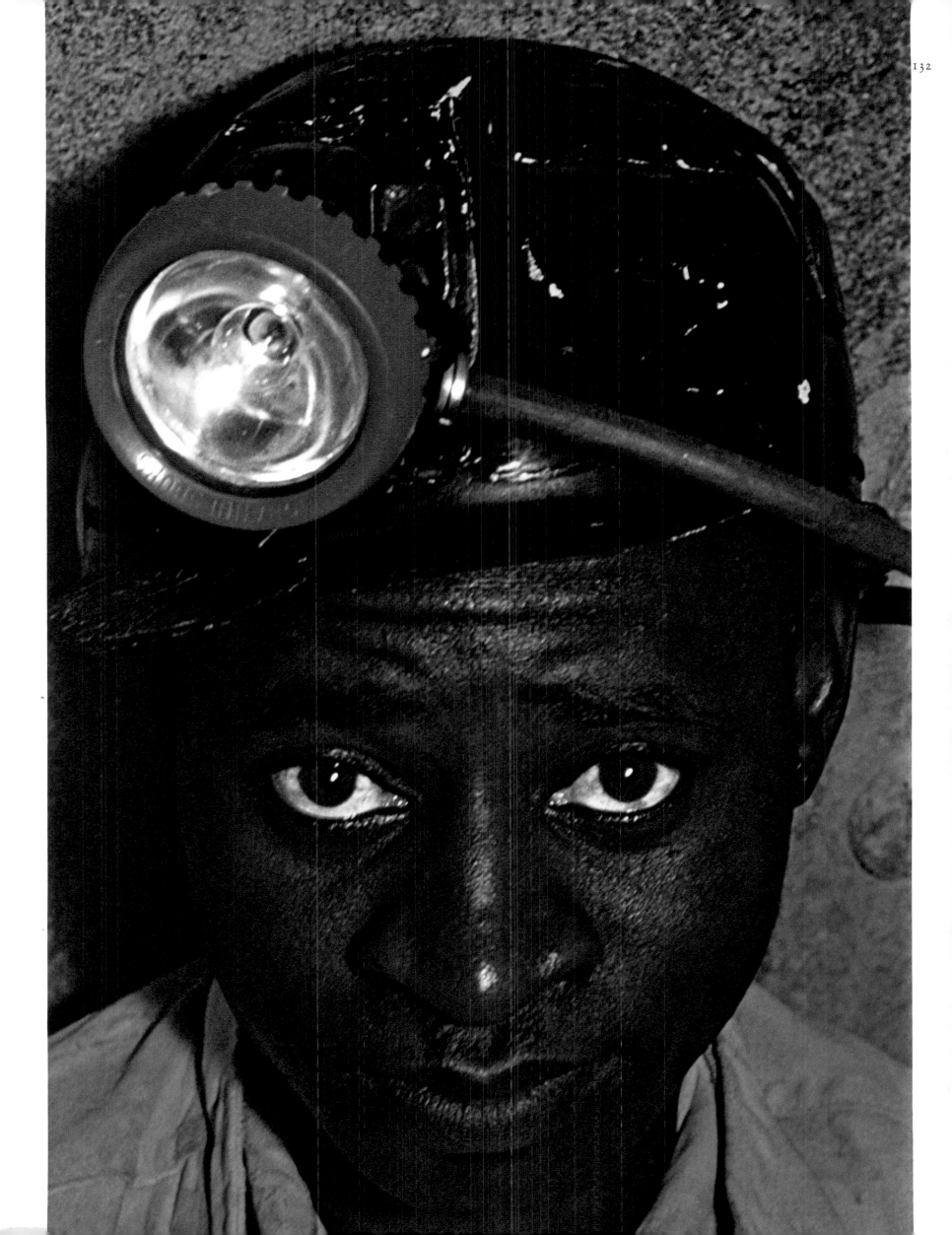

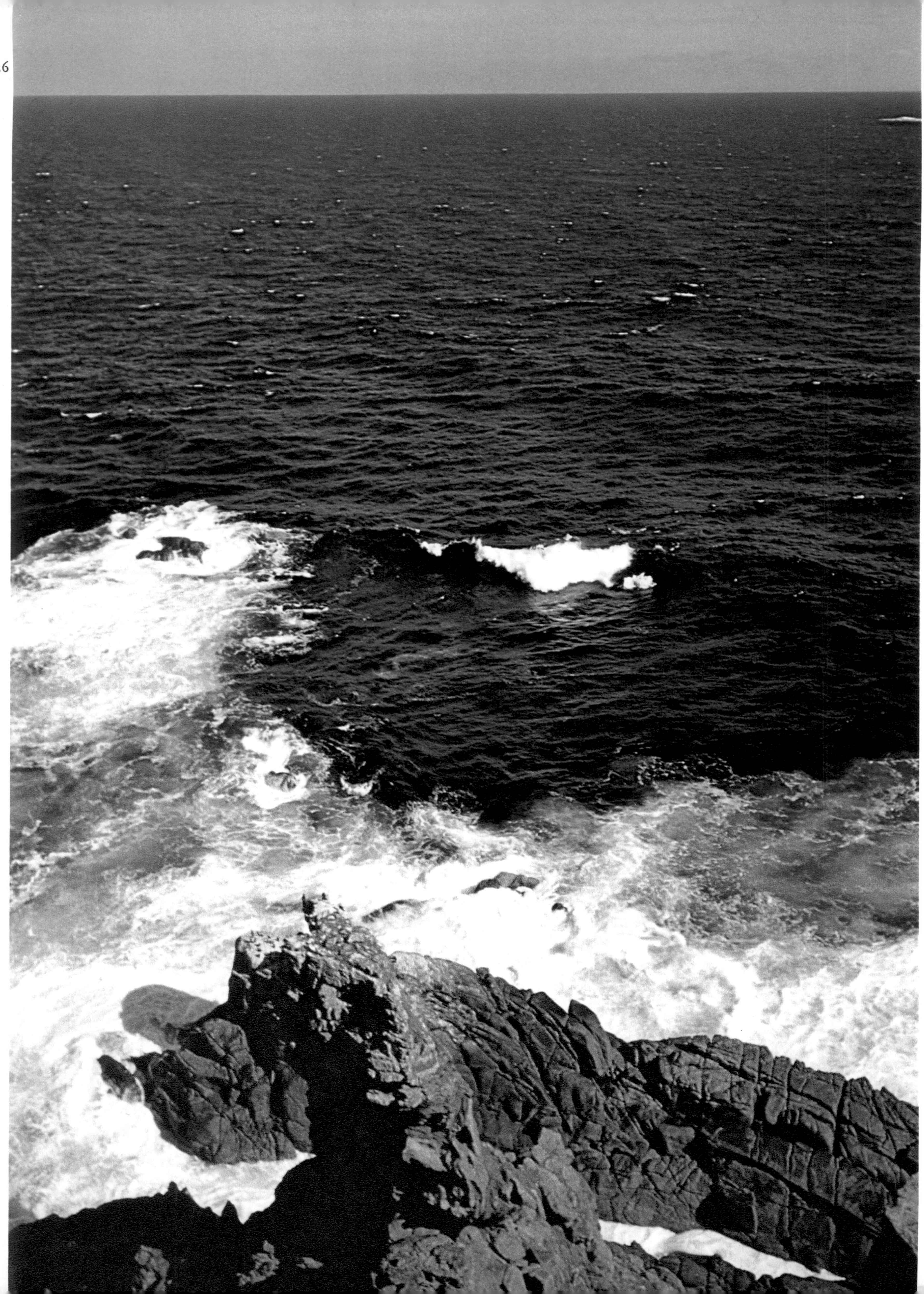

Africa for various black tribes and to give these areas, these Bantustans, gradually increasing autonomy—with economic and technical support from South Africa—so that they can ultimately be completely self-governing.

134 *Bhaka man in the Transkei, Republic of South Africa.* The Bhaka, a tribe of the Fingu group, belong to the Bantu-speaking population, and have migrated from the north to their present-day settlement on the Great Kei River. It is remarkable what an undisturbed life these tribes are able to lead in their own territory: the utopian ideal of the positive side of racial segregation.

135 *Xhosa woman near Idutgwa, Transkei, Republic of South Africa.*

136 *The Cape of Good Hope, Republic of South Africa.* Here where the waters of the Atlantic join the waves of the Indian Ocean, the seafarer faces an uncomfortable voyage. Without sighting the African coast, Bartholomew Diaz sailed past the Cape in 1487 or 1488, his ship battered and driven by storms. Not until the return trip did he sight land and, due to his past experience, he named it the "Cape of Storms." But his navigator-king, John II of Portugal, hoping to make Portugal's fortune from this new spice route to the Indies, rechristened it "Cape of Good Hope." On a later journey Diaz went down with his ship not far from here, thus calling in question the royal formulation. Following Diaz' course, Vasco da Gama then also sailed to the Far East, and from the fifteenth century down to the present, the southernmost crags of Africa have always been an important landmark for navigators.

Emil Birrer

Notes

My two books of photographs, *Africa—from the Mediterranean to the Equator* and *Africa—From the Equator to the Cape of Good Hope* (which appeared in one volume entitled *Africa* in the English language edition) were first published twelve years ago and appeared in several languages. A few years later they were already out of print. However, the continuing interest that has been shown in these books over the years has now led us to publish a new edition. The choice of a larger format and a new layout have enabled me to concentrate on the most striking photographic records. At the same time, I have tightened the thematic content to give a picture of the overwhelming diversity of the African landscape, the remarkable wildlife of this continent, and the fascinating world of its African inhabitants. The photographic material for the present volume was collected in 1955/56 when I spent ten months traversing the African continent from north to south with Otto Lehmann of the Swiss Broadcasting Corporation. He kept an account of our travels and wrote the captions for the first edition. The captions in this new edition are intended primarily for general information, and most of the original descriptive material has gone. However, so that the reader may still have a taste of the adventure involved in this great journey, I am including a few of our experiences in these notes.

Since the publication of the first edition, I have often been asked questions about our travels, problems of photography, and other matters. I am, therefore, taking advantage of the opportunity to go into some of these questions here, particularly those which are still of interest today. Typical examples of these questions are: "How did you manage to find your way through the uncharted regions of the desert?" "What cameras did you work with and how did you protect your equipment in the desert and in the tropics?" "How did you solve the problem of food?" "How were you accepted by the Africans?" "Were you ever attacked by a lion or by other wild animals?" "What were the most beautiful, the most difficult, the most impressive moments during your trip?"

First: "*How did you manage to find your way through the uncharted regions of the desert?*"   Crossing the Libyan desert between Fezzan and the Tibesti Mountains was perhaps the most difficult part of the undertaking as far as our vehicles were concerned. Our goal in traversing this part of the desert was to reach a certain place at a certain time; namely, to arrive at longitude 21° 05′ east and latitude 20° 40′ north, where I wanted to photograph the rare phenomenon of an annular eclipse. Since large tracts in this part of the desert led through no-man's-land, it would have been irresponsible to undertake the trek with only one vehicle. We therefore added a second vehicle with four-wheel drive for the first fifty days of the journey. This second Willys station wagon driven by Ernst Joos and Marcel Chappot was rebuilt so that it could carry 135 gallons of petrol and 60 gallons of water. But even this reserve supply of fuel was insufficient to guarantee getting us across the most difficult section of the no-man's-land between the el-

Gatroun Oasis and Zouar on the western edge of the Tibesti Mountains. This trek covering more than eight hundred miles was to take us through endless stretches of stony wastes and rocky deserts, across which we had to drive in the first gear of the low ratio gears, and this of course required three or four times the amount of petrol normally required.

Months in advance I had made every effort to gather information about our planned route, but I waited in vain for answers to the various letters that I had written to officials in towns, oases and military outposts situated along the route. I finally learned through other sources that from time to time during the winter months, a transport firm in Tunis sent out trucks along sections of the route we intended to take. These trucks supplied isolated oases and military posts with food and fuel. (A few years ago, the company discontinued these runs.) We made an agreement by letter that the convoy leaving about ten days before our arrival in Tunis would take along a fifty gallon tank of petrol to be deposited at a place called Bazelaire, which consisted of a small, uninhabited tin hut which had been especially constructed as an emergency outpost for the convoys. This hut was situated approximately mid-way in the 800-mile stretch of no-man's-land and it was, therefore, essential that we find it.

Upon arriving in Tunis, we asked the director of the transport firm to inspect our vehicles to ensure that they were adequately equipped for the trek. He had nothing but praise for our preparations, only criticizing our cross-country tyres, which had been recommended to us in Switzerland, and suggesting we use summer tyres with an ordinary tread, since they do not dig into the sand as the others do. As tyres in Tunisia were extremely expensive at the time, we decided to put summer tyres on only one of the vehicles.

The director was unable to tell us how to reach Bazelaire, because there are no detailed maps of the region. When I think back on the adventure now, I must admit that we really put our trust in God when we set off to find our tank of petrol at Bazelaire; it was like looking for a needle in a haystack. After leaving the main road on the Mediterranean coast, we set our compass, which was built into the car, at 180° south. We were especially dependent upon this instrument when we had to drive round sections of mountains, and the tracks made by the trucks were also confusing, since the convoys, as we had been warned in Tunis, took a different route with every run. Moreover, on the long stretches of rock and stone, even trucks weighing ten tons did not make the least impression. This drive across endless rocky plains, across stones burnt black by the sun and worn to razor sharp edges, was exceedingly wearing for our vehicles. It was no surprise when we occasionally came across bits and pieces of wreckage.

We had made every effort during our preparations to guarantee our safety so far as we could. Swissair had been kind enough to agree to my request and put a radio at our disposal with which we could send out SOS signals in case of emergency. The military outposts located in the area at that time were in radio contact with each other and were to be kept informed of our movements. It was agreed that we could use the radio daily between 11:00 and 11:15, to send out SOS signals, should we run into difficulties.

According to the regulations, our two Willys station wagons were allowed a maximum additional weight of 1440 pounds. But by the time we were ready to set off from Tunis, with full loads of water, petrol and food, we had far exceeded this limit. Our weight on an official weigh-bridge in Tunis came to a further 2660 pounds for each car. We were concerned about this excessive overweight and breathed a sigh of relief every time our cars survived a particularly difficult and exacting day's drive. There were days when we only covered thirty to thirty-five miles from early morning to nightfall, creeping over the rocks at a walking pace—those days are unforgettable. Again and again the strength of all four men was required to heave rocks out of the way so that we could continue.

Although we had barely imagined the hardships in store for our vehicles, we had fortunately had a strong material wrapped round the springs before leaving Switzerland. Our purpose in doing this had been to prevent the sand from collecting between the plates of the springs. Not until long after our trek across the desert was over did we have the opportunity to have our Willys completely overhauled in Nairobi. (Our friends, Ernst and Marcel, drove the other car home along the 'Bidon 5' route, situated in the western part of the Sahara.) Who would ever have guessed that this bandaging around the springs would not only prevent the sand from filtering into them, but would also keep several spring plates which had broken in two from falling apart completely. It must have happened early on in the desert, when we were still struggling over dunes. This cost us a great deal of time, because we had to dig paths for our cars over each dune. We soon discovered how to avoid this time-consuming task: First we climbed the sand dune on foot to determine where it was the hardest, then we drove towards that particular spot at full speed to gain enough impetus to bump over the crest of the dune. Only later did we learn that our spring plates were no match for this rough treatment. By changing the tyres on at least one of our cars, we saved ourselves a good deal of time and frustration. As soon as we came to the first particularly difficult spots, we realized how useless the cross-country tyres were. They dug deeper and deeper into the soft sand like shovels, whereas ordinary tyres tend to skim over the top.

Second: *"What cameras did you work with and how did you protect your equipment in the desert and in the tropics?"* I had already gathered some experience from earlier trips through Africa and on other continents. But it was obvious from the very beginning that this African trip, in the course of which our station wagons were to cover 22,500 miles, would exact the maximum from our cameras and film equipment. After the rugged trip across the desert, our equipment was subjected to the hot and humid climate of the Congolese rain forests and also had to be transported up high mountains by African carriers. Because of the optical advantages of 35 mm photography and because of weight problems connected with more extensive equipment, I decided to work primarily with the Leica M-3: three M-3 bodies, as well as 35 mm, 50 mm, 90 mm, 135 mm and 400 mm Leica lenses and various accessories.

I also had a Fish-Eye camera, which I had rigged up myself. I intended to use it for certain ideas I had about photographing the path of the sun at the equator. In addition I took along another "home-made" camera which had a focal length of 1500 mm. We nicknamed this seven foot monster "fat Bertha." It was constructed so that it could be connected to a 4/5-inch camera, a 6/6-back wall, and to the Leica as well. We used it very seldom, however, because it was so hard to handle; two men were required to mount it on its revolving tripod that had been specially constructed for the occasion. Because the Leica is so handy and is ready to use at a moment's notice, the lion's share of the work on this trip was done with our Leica equipment, i.e. 130 out of the total 136 pictures in this book. The following story serves to illustrate the great advantages of a 35 mm camera.

When we first visited the Victoria Falls the Zambezi was in flood. The clouds of spray were so thick that we were never able to see the entire width of the falls at one time. The incessant shower caused me some concern when I had chosen a particularly exposed spot from which to operate or was planning to put the large 4/5-inch camera into action. At the Main Fall I cautiously made my way across the slippery, sodden slope to the edge of the perpendicular cliff, trying to find solid ground for the outer leg of the tripod. Long before I succeeded, I was already soaked to the skin, since the up-current of the roaring, crashing masses of water dashed the spray squarely on top of me. Between two gusts of spray, I finally managed to mount the Graphic View on to the tripod and immediately covered it with a black cloth. But a few drops of water had spattered the lens in spite of all my efforts—and of course my glasses were wet too. After wiping my glasses and the lens, I quickly checked the focusing screen, by which time the lens was already covered with spray again. After several tries, cleaning the lens each time, I finally succeeded in focusing the camera. By that time the black cloth was dripping wet and I was standing in water up to my ankles. At long last a couple of dry seconds, but just at that moment the falls themselves disappeared behind a curtain of water. Immediately, the wind rose again and once more I was covered with spray. There was not a dry square inch on my body and since I had nothing left with which to wipe either glasses or lens, I was forced to give up. But the spot I had chosen was ideal; I went through the same procedure on the following day, hoping that the wind would change direction. This time I was armed with a raincoat and my entire supply of handkerchiefs. However, wind and water played the same game all over again. I began to wonder if I should give up entirely. No. The following morning I left the 4/5-inch camera and tripod in the car, and set off with two of the Leicas tucked under my raincoat. Like lightning I had the camera ready, took the shot, and tucked the instrument away again. Within a quarter of an hour I had shot all the pictures I wanted.

We also visited several game reserves and had to make very careful preparations to photograph the animals in their natural habitat. From earlier visits to African game reserves, I had learned that photographing out of the window of an ordinary car was far from ideal. On the roof of the Willys station wagon, which is already a high car, I had a special structure erected, based on plans I had drawn earlier. Thanks to this, I was able to climb directly from the driver's seat on to the roof of the car, where there was a large metal ring a little over three feet in diameter. The telephoto lenses with the Leica could then be attached to a sliding-carriage which was in turn fixed to the metal ring. Like a soldier on a gun-carriage, I was now able to turn with the camera in any direction desired, and from this high stand it was not only possible to get an excellent view in all directions, but also to photograph animals in tall grass. Our structure, for which we were so often envied, did not adhere one hundred percent to the official regulations according to which it was forbidden to leave the inside of the car while in the reserve. Many a warden and gamekeeper overlooked our high stand when we drove by. But anyone who thinks it was fun sitting up there from before sunrise until after dusk is mistaken. It was exhausting work sitting in the searing sun all day long, plagued by innumerable insects, bent over and peering into the viewfinder for hours on end, sometimes spending the whole day waiting in vain for a spectacular shot.

With special permission and accompanied by conservationists or gamewardens, we were often able to leave the car and stalk the animals on foot. I remember my first encounter with a wild animal in Africa as if it were yesterday. It was in Garamba Park, a game reserve in the northern part of the Congo, which is closed to the public and used exclusively for scientific study. We were standing in the back of our small truck with three Africans. There was only one narrow track leading northwards in the direction of the Sudanese border. The White rhinoceros and the Reticulated giraffe are specialities of Garamba Park. Captain Micha, who is a conservationist, told us we would need a good bit of luck if we were to see a White rhinoceros; an American visitor had recently spent two weeks on the look-out without success. We had been under way for an hour and nothing very exciting had happened. Suddenly an African pointed to the left and in the distance we recognized some cow antelopes behind a few bushes. Captain Micha suggested that we stalk them on foot. It had never occurred to me that we should be allowed to leave our vehicle, and the invitation came as a surprise. But I climbed out of the truck and crawled towards the antelopes, trying to keep under cover as much as possible. The animals had noticed me and were eyeing me as I set up the 400 mm Telyt in the fork of a tree. (I had unfortunately left the tripod behind.) The luxuriant foliage obstructed the view, and by the time I was ready the antelopes had vanished. So, back to the car.

Did something move over there when I turned? Something big and grey? Was it a boulder over there? A boulder here? No—it moved again—a horn—a rhinoceros! Amazed, I stood rooted to the spot, and like a flash remembered having read somewhere that a rhinoceros attacks head on. I observed that the grey blotched rhinoceros had not scented me yet, but was eating grass with its head lowered and was moving straight towards me step by step. Would I make it to the truck? Where was the truck anyway?

At that moment something cracked behind me; I hardly dared turn my head, but it was one of the men from the truck. My friends had seen the rhinoceros and had sent the African to see to my safety and to reassure me. He smiled, and with signs indicated that we could still take a few steps towards the animal—I firmly refused. I motioned to him to bend over so that I could rest the telephoto lens on his back, since I could not hold it unsupported. In the meantime, the enormous animal still had not scented us, and had come so close that its monstrous head filled the entire view-finder. I took the picture. Suddenly the rhinoceros raised its head; it had heard the click of the camera. Was it going to attack us? I found the tension unbearable, but the African, still bending over, turned and grinned at me. We stood absolutely immobile for a few seconds, then the animal lowered its head and continued grazing.

In reference to photographic equipment, one important consideration is how quickly and efficiently it is ready for action. Our equipment was, of course, packed in bags and small cases for excursions on foot and up mountains. Knapsacks are not to be recommended, as the natives always carry burdens on their heads. To store the equipment in the station wagon itself we had constructed a system of drawers, and since our apparatus was always put away in the same place thanks to foam-rubber cushioning, everything we needed was handy at a moment's notice. To prevent the drawers from rattling and shaking during the trip, we fixed them to the floor of the car with elastic straps. This worked successfully even under the roughest conditions. During our trip across the desert, temperatures could range in one day from 115 °F in the shade at noon to 20 °F at night. But because the desert air is so dry, even such extreme variations did not damage the film. The only problem was the fine sand in the air which managed to find its way into the most unlikely places. This was a serious problem, as the sand can cause damaging vertical scratch marks when the shutter is cocked. It is therefore advisable to wrap the apparatus in plastic bags at the approach of a sandstorm. Cameras and lenses should be examined every evening and any dust or sand that may have seeped in should be removed with a soft brush. What is more difficult, however, is the storage of film for any length of time—especially colour film—in humid tropical regions. (I used Kodachrome for colour, and Ilford Pan F, FP 3, and HP 3 for black and white.) Unexposed film wrapped in a special vacuum-pack for the tropics is not affected by climatic conditions. Exposed film, on the other hand, should be developed as quickly as possible. I therefore always tried to send exposed colour film to Switzerland by air to be developed. In certain areas where air freight could not be counted on, I used the following method to store exposed colour film. I had taken along a number of containers which could be, as it were, hermetically sealed. Little cloth bags filled with dry crystals, Silica gel, were sewn into these containers. The Silica gel would absorb any moisture which might penetrate the containers. When the Silica gel crystals have absorbed to capacity, they become pale pink, and can be made active again by carefully heating the grains to dry them out, thus restoring them to their original deep blue colour. When the Africans watched me "toasting" the Silica gel in the Congo jungle and saw it change from a pale pink to a deep dark blue before their very eyes, they must have thought I was a magician. They never tired of watching this procedure.

If no Silica gel is available, I am given to understand from an authoritative source that dry rice can also produce the same effect. Whether it was due to these precautions or not, not one of the approximately ten thousand exposures that I made during the ten months' journey was damaged by climatic conditions. This does not mean, of course, that travellers in Africa must take precautions like these. If one plans to be under way for only three or four weeks, then the usual precautionary measures should suffice, though the film should be developed immediately upon returning.

Third: "*How did you solve the problem of food?*"   For the first fifty days of the trek across the desert we survived primarily on canned goods, varying them as frequently as possible with rice or noodles of some kind. Later on, too, in order to save time, we rarely prepared fresh food; canned goods clearly dominated our diet. This lack of fresh vegetables probably caused the virulent boils with which I was plagued from time to time.

One thing is certain: members of expeditions to uncivilized parts of the world do well to have strong stomachs, because not infrequently one finds oneself sitting before a dish that is hardly the daily fare to which one's stomach and palate are accustomed. I remember one evening on the Logone River in Chad. We had reached Katoa just before sunset. The palace of an Arab, named Aksalai, "Chef du Canton Katoa," stands on a square surrounded by giant trees behind high mud walls. We had intended to stay at the guest-house in front of the palace gates, but it was so musty and damp that we decided to set up our tent outside. While doing this in the dusk, we were offered two calabash gourds. The thick cow's milk, in which a few bits of straw and some dung were floating about, was a token of friendship from Aksalai. In the early morning we managed to throw the milk, which had already turned sour, into the river unnoticed. Shortly afterwards another gift arrived from Aksalai: more milk again garnished with a bit of dung, and in addition some plum-sized eggs which had already begun to develop embryos. This time we had no choice but to gulp down these offerings in the presence of Aksalai's emissaries.

Fourth: "*How were you accepted by the Africans?*"   On our first trip together in the Congo we had a small truck with a driver at our disposal. The driver, whose name was Kilimbazo, was a tall, good-looking Congolese who spoke some French. After a few days' drive we arrived at a missionary settlement in the northern part of the Congo, where we were received most cordially by the Belgian priests there. One of them promptly engaged us in conversation and, obviously astonished, asked us how we had come across our driver. The youth had been in his class in school for a time and he knew him very well. Did we realize that Kilimbazo had commited a felony and had been in prison for some time? We tried to ignore this unpleasant revelation and agreed not to mention it to Kilimbazo. We trusted him implicitly as we had before, and during the several weeks that we travelled together, had no difficulties at all.

The Belgian administrator of a game reserve, who had lived alone among Africans for many years, told us the following story about his experiences with Africans. One day a substantial sum of money had to be taken to the bank in the nearest city. The administrator trusted his employees and asked one of his subordinates to take the money to the bank for him. This meant a five to six days' round trip on foot. After six days, the African had not returned. The Belgian simply thought that he had probably taken advantage of the opportunity to visit his relatives in the vicinity. After ten days had passed, he began to be worried, but mentioned the situation to no one. The man finally came back a little over two weeks later in poor condition. On the second day after he had left, he had been taken ill and, suffering from a high fever, had managed to struggle to his relatives, where he remained until the attacks of fever had subsided. Thereupon, he had returned to the reserve with the little cloth bag into which the money had been sewn still hanging round his neck under his shirt.

At Bengamisa in the Congo, we turned off the main road and entered the jungle, driving towards the west. The route was very narrow and in poor condition; long stretches were under water, and we had impenetrable jungle to our left and right, with a heavy dark roof of leaves, above which the last peals of thunder from a passing thunderstorm echoed. There must recently have been a severe storm because uprooted trees were obstructing the route. Fortunately, the tree trunks blocking our way were not too large; trunks eight inches thick offered quite sufficient resistance to our axes, for the wood was as hard as iron. We would probably have had to struggle for quite a long time if a half-naked African had not appeared at that moment. Smiling, he took the axe away from us and with a few expert strokes cleared the path. Before we even had a chance to show our gratitude, he had already vanished into the jungle again.

But to complete the picture I must also relate a series of events that occurred in Tanzania. We had been invited to spend the night with a Swiss couple who lived well off the beaten path, several hours by car from the nearest settlement. At nightfall, our host lit several floor lamps which were placed in a row in front of the large windows of the house, so that they lit up the world outside. When we asked what this was for our host informed us that a thief was known to be in the vicinity and the lights were intended to blind him. This was the best means of self-defence. After dinner our host conducted us to the guest house, which was some two hundred feet away from his own. There he handed us a loaded revolver, and said that we should shoot immediately if someone tried to enter our room, so as to alarm his people. Although we did not take the matter very seriously at first, sleeping was out of the question. All night we heard steps outside, which were probably simply the men on guard duty. In any case nothing happened, and we left again the following noon.

A few months later, after we had returned home from our journey, I received a letter from our hosts, in which they told us the history of the thief, who had also been wanted for murder. After many thefts and robberies and finally several murders as well, Osale, as he was called, had come into possession of some rifles, a sub-machine gun, and a good deal of ammunition. He then joined up with a few other men, and in the end he even had a car. The local population provided cover for this band of robbers partly out of fear, but also because Osale was believed to possess magic powers. Osale was so audacious that he often boasted publicly about a robbery even before he had carried it out. On the day of our expected visit, our host had in fact been warned by various Africans in the neighbourhood that an attempt on his house was planned for that very night. The attack was in fact called off because of the arrival of two strangers in a car during the afternoon—us! Our station wagon with its construction on top on which a machine-gun could well have been mounted instead of a telephoto lens must have impressed even Osale. After his gang succeeded in breaking into a different house every evening for a whole week, the police were finally informed of Osale's hideout. He was hunted down by a military patrol and shot as he was trying to escape.

Fifth: *"Were you ever attacked by a lion or by other wild animals?"* Facing a wild animal unprotected is probably a memorable experience for anyone. In the process of taking photographs in game reserves in various areas all over the continent, we had occasion to encounter elephants, lions, buffaloes, and other wild animals on foot. But that first moment when one suddenly finds oneself face to face with a large wild animal always makes the biggest impression. I saw free roaming lions for the first time in Albert Park during our first trip to the Congo. It was noon and oppressively hot; we were driving across the Rwindi plain on our way out of the reserve, a bit depressed, not because of the enervating heat and the thirst, but because we had failed to sight the "King of the Bush," the lion. Otto was frustrated too, and for a change, was driving our small truck himself. I was in the back with an African park warden. Nothing was happening; nothing moved in the broiling midday sun.

There! As if electrified, both the African and I shouted "Lion!" and I banged on the top of the cab with my fist. This was our signal to stop immediately. A lion had just leapt across our route about two hundred yards ahead of us. We had managed to get a glimpse of it for about two seconds. We waited in vain. What should we do? We drove some one hundred yards closer to the spot where the lion had disappeared into the thick undergrowth, and there we remained immobile for five minutes, ten minutes—nothing.

We asked the warden if he would not reconnoitre for us with the binoculars. He finally came running back after fifteen minutes and told us that he had located the lion, but that we could only get there on foot. None of us was armed. Carrying weapons is strictly forbidden in all the game reserves. The three of us carefully stalked through the dense undergrowth. Finally the African stood still and pointed through the foliage to an isolated palm bush under which one could see something brown. I motioned to him that we were not in a very good position. I could only get a satisfactory shot if we moved to the edge of the bushes in which we were hiding. The moment had come when I had to decide between going out in the open and facing the lion or going home empty-handed. In order to avoid all noise, I set up the tripod and mounted the telephoto lens first. Only then did I venture out of our hiding place, immediately setting down the tripod and peering into the viewfinder. A lioness was lying under a bush, probably taking a nap. No, she had seen me. First shot. She jumped up. Second shot. She was coming towards me. Third shot. Still looking into the viewfinder, I shouted excitedly to my friends in the bushes behind me to stay put. The lioness had come still closer. Fourth shot. And just as the shutter clicked, I saw her veer sharply to the left and disappear into the bush. The whole process must have taken no more than five seconds; but my knees felt wobbly long afterwards.

In Uganda we visited the Murchison Falls Game Reserve on the Victoria Nile. This area is renowned for its crocodiles, whose favourite haunts can be reached by taking the small motorboat, *Oribi,* upstream. With gaping jaws these twelve to fifteen foot monsters lie on the sandy banks of the river or on grassy islands in the middle. Since crocodiles have an extremely keen sense of hearing, we tried to approach these giant dozing reptiles without making a sound. We turned the engine off and let the boat drift towards the shore at a bend in the river. Here we could see a magnificent specimen in the shade of a tree. The animal was lying there motionless, its wide-open jaws revealing a wreath of pointed teeth. I tried to adjust the camera as silently as possible, but I had to be quick with the first shot, because soon the current would drive the boat too close to shore. The boat brushed the shore almost at the same time that I released the shutter of the Leica. Whether it was the click of the shutter or the movement of the boat, the creature streaked out of the thicket like lightning and disappeared into the water within inches of our boat, causing such large waves that we had all we could do not to fall overboard.

Sixth: "*What were the most beautiful, the most difficult, the most impressive moments of your trip?*" In the course of our exhausting drive into the heart of the Tibesti Mountains, we came to the valley of Gonoa—a fantastic world of rocks and boulders. These giants populate the plain like a stage set: red chunks worn into weird shapes by heat and cold. Looking for recently discovered rock drawings, witnesses to a prehistoric era, we climbed across the colourful rocky plain. Then… what an experience! To find oneself suddenly face to face with a life-size representation of an elephant scratched into a wall of rock by people who lived there thousands of years ago, when the now barren desert of rock must still have been a fertile plain.

We lived through one of our most difficult moments in the Royal Natal National Park in South Africa, almost at the end of our trip, when our station wagon with everything in it nearly went up in flames. On that particular day, I had taken a drive before breakfast as usual, because the light conditions are always best in the early morning. We drove towards the end of the valley, approaching the "Monts aux Sources," a magnificent group of mountains that circle the end of the valley like an amphitheatre. We knew that we could not drive very far with the station wagon, since the engine was only running on three cylinders, and we would have to find a garage immediately afterwards. We drove a few miles downhill along a narrow little road, which then became so steep and poor that we parked the car in some tall dry grass and continued on foot through some woods, finally coming to a rise from which there was a breath-taking panorama. But we also saw dark smoke rising in the direction from which we had just come. The smoke increased and then began to spread rapidly in such a way that it could only be a grass fire which had apparently just started. Thick clouds of smoke moving towards us indicated that the wind was blowing the blaze in our direction. We were very concerned. We hurried through the woods to a spot from which we could see the station wagon. The sight almost made our hearts stop: the station wagon was perhaps five hundred yards away from us and right behind it was a huge wall of fire running straight across the valley and steadily closing in on our vehicle. I made a dash for the car, tripping over holes hidden in the ground, struggling through the tall, dry grass; in the thick stinging smoke I suddenly caught sight of four black figures, one of them on horseback, excitedly trying to get into the locked car. They saw me and shouted, "The key! The key!" With a last effort I reached the car. The wall of fire was already within a few yards of it. The man on horseback indicated that there was only one way out—to drive up the mountain. I stepped on the accelerator, but the engine was slow to pick up because the car was only running on three cylinders. I let it roll back towards the fire again to get a better start and finally managed to start moving slowly uphill using the low ratio gear. The fire had already overtaken us on the right, so we had to drive alongside it. The African rider galloped on ahead of us and pointed to a piece of land which was still smoking from the fire that had already swept through it. Here I stopped the car, while the popping, crackling wall of fire raged past our "island."
Exhausted and lost in thought, we drove through the charred landscape back to camp and breakfast. There we learned that the fire had been deliberately started early in the morning. It had never occurred to anyone that someone could be driving about up there so early in the day.

An Austrian landscape painter, who was eating his breakfast at a table next to ours, was not at all delighted that someone had set fire to the entire area. He had started painting a picture the previous afternoon. "How can I go on painting here now?" he said to us. "All that is left of the landscape is a charred mess."

The most impressive and also most dangerous undertaking during our journey was the descent into the active crater of the Nyiragongo Volcano, the only volcano in the world that has a permanent lake of molten lava. We stayed there for several days. The Nyiragongo is one of the chain of the Virunga volcanoes and lies a bit south of the equator in Congo-Kinshasa, not far from the border of Uganda. André Meyer, the volcanologist who was with us, organized a whole troop of Africans to transport our voluminous equipment to the top of the 11,500 foot high volcano—our scientific measuring apparatus, photographic equipment, camping supplies, and a heavy cable-coil. The next step was to climb down the steep wall of the crater in order to set up our bivouac for the following day on the lower platform. Otto had to give up because of breathing difficulties, and returned to the base camp with the carriers. When the fog had lifted a little, André Meyer and I climbed down the 600 foot cliff at an angle of 70 degrees. In preparation for the descent, we had thrown a 300 foot safety rope over the edge of the crater and had fastened it to a large boulder. The lava formations were extremely eroded, loose and rotten in parts. With each new hold and step that we took, smaller and larger bits of rock broke away from the wall, so that we had to stay very close to each other while climbing. Even the safety rope, which afforded somewhat more security at particularly critical spots, occasionally caused fragments to crumble off the wall, which came hurtling by at frightening speed, flying past our heads down what looked to us like a perfectly perpendicular wall as we were climbing. It was a good thing that André Meyer had thought of taking steel helmets along. When we had reached the end of the safety rope, we had already covered more than half the distance, but now we had to manage the rest without the assurance of a safety rope. After about another hundred feet, the wall gradually became less steep. Finally at the bottom, André Meyer told me that only about a dozen people had ever undertaken the descent before. Having found the end of the cable which André had previously swung down over the edge of the crater, we pulled it towards the middle of the platform and secured it in a crevice on the jagged surface of the shelf, rolling a heavy chunk of lava on top of it for extra security. Then André gave the two Africans who had stayed behind on the upper lip of the crater a signal to tauten the cable on the winch which he had anchored securely on the top. The construction was ready. Now tent, sleeping bags, and cooking utensils could be lowered down to us. By this time it was fairly late and we had to finish setting up our bivouac by the light of a kerosene lantern.

There was a thick fog the following morning. We could not see ten steps ahead of us, but our bivouac was about two hundred feet from the cable. Since one always has to take fog into account at these altitudes in a humid tropical zone, I had taken the precaution of laying out aluminium poles in a straight line to mark the distance between our bivouac and the cable. The two Africans who had made the one hour's descent to the base camp the night before were already on the rim of the crater again early the next morning. Visibility was zero and we had to communicate by means of shouted signals. It took us until the early afternoon to get all our equipment down to the lower shelf. Not only all our equipment but also every drop of water had to be transported by this tedious method. And the water, too, had to be carried up from the base camp. Therefore, not until early evening of the second day did we have a chance to take a look at our surroundings and venture out towards the middle of the circular shelf, from which we could finally get the long awaited view of the inside of the crater with its lake of molten lava. The lava lake had once been the height of the shelf on which we were camping. Solidified waves of lava traverse the surface of the platform which becomes increasingly crumbly and fragmented towards the centre where the walls of the crater drop vertically into the molten lake. For the final thirty-five feet, we proceeded on our stomachs, slowly creeping over the rugged surface, until we were at long last able to peer over the verge of the abyss.

What a fantastic, what an unbelievable sight! The yellow-red glowing lava lake bubbled and boiled beneath us like a monstrous witch's cauldron. Stinging fumes of sulphur and tremendous heat wafted up into our faces. Huge fountains of fire exploded on the surface, spurted high into the air, and then fell hissing back into the glowing lake. Myriads of lines—like a gigantic, glowing spider's web—were in constant motion, creating ghost-like patterns on the surface of the lake. Again and again fountains of fire broke through the surface and hurled gleaming golden waves of lava against the walls of the crater. From time to time we had to withdraw our heads—the heat and the sulphur fumes rising from this inferno were too strong for us. The moment we retreated from the edge of the perpendicular walls of the crater, heat and sulphur disappeared; one could breathe fresh air again. For a long, long time we lay there gazing down into the depths of hell, hardly noticing that night had already fallen over us. We returned to the tent.

During the three nights that we spent there I was unable to sleep. The impression was so overwhelming, the experience so intense; it was like sitting on the powder keg of the universe; it was like feeling the pulse of the earth.

Neither the first edition nor this new edition would have been possible without the support of many individuals and institutions. My first thought, my first expression of gratitude belongs to those who accompanied me on the journey: Otto Lehmann, Marcel Chappot, and Ernst Joos. Otto and Marcel will not be able to witness the publication of this new edition. Marcel Chappot died unexpectedly from the consequences of a serious illness. Otto Lehmann was a passenger in the airplane which crashed into Mount Marra in the Djebel Tereng above the Sudan in May, 1960. None of the passengers on this charter flight survived.

I thank Conzett & Huber in Zürich for handing over the copyrights. I am grateful to Mr Alfred E. Herzer for his efforts in bringing about this edition. I owe special thanks to Dr Bruno Mariacher, whose help effected a break-through on the international level.

Again I wish to thank Professor Dr Heini Hediger and Mr and Mrs John and Lucie Tanner for their help. I thank Professor Dr Emil Egli for his textual contribution, *The Continent of Africa,* and Emil Birrer, who prepared the new captions. I wish to thank Ingrid Parge, Walter Glättli, Fritz Hofer, and Hans Frei for their help in publishing this work. The tireless work of the management of the photogravure firm, Imago, Zürich, and of the specialists in photogravure printing, ensured that this book was faultlessly produced. Ernst Gerbig, with whom I checked the colour proofs, made a substantial contribution to the faithful colour of the reproductions. The Papierfabrik Biberist made the paper, Regina-Druck in Zürich printed the text, and the Buchbinderei Burkhardt in Zürich executed the binding. These have all contributed to the faultless production of this book.

Forch/Zürich, Autumn 1969   *Emil Schulthess*

List of Illustrations

Southern Africa